Sun, Fun
and Crowds
SEASIDE HOLIDAYS BETWEEN THE WARS

1 Beach huts and deck chairs at Bournemouth today, little different from those used by holidaymakers in the 1930s. (Diane Harris)

Sun, Fun
and Crowds

SEASIDE HOLIDAYS BETWEEN THE WARS

STEVEN BRAGGS AND DIANE HARRIS

TEMPUS

First published 2000

PUBLISHED BY:

Tempus Publishing Ltd
The Mill, Brimscombe Port
Stroud, Gloucestershire GL5 2QG

British Library Cataloguing in Publication Data.
A catalogue record for this book is available from the British Library.

ISBN 0 7524 1891 2

Typesetting and origination by Tempus Publishing.
PRINTED AND BOUND IN GREAT BRITAIN.

*The design for the front cover is taken from a guide to Margate, Cliftonville, Westbrook, Birchington
and Westgate-on-Sea from the 1930s. (Thanet District Council)*
The photograph on the back cover is thought to be of Margate beach during the 1930s.

Contents

Acknowledgements

The authors would like to acknowledge the help and support given by the following:

Blackpool Library, The Bodleian Library, Oxford, Kevin Boorman (Hastings Borough Council), Bournemouth Library, Julia Braggs, Brighton Library, Roger Bristow and the staff of Hastings Library, Anne-Marie Chatterton (Ford Motor Company), Beverley Cole (Curator, National Railway Museum, York), Paula Colyer (Thanet District Council), David Crundwell (Vauxhall Motors), Dominic Delaney (Isle of Man Department of Tourism & Leisure), Eastbourne Library, Elsie Floyd, Francis & E. Margaret Harris, Martin J. Harris, Sue Hodgson (Newquay's Tourism & Marketing Officer), Jeremy's (Oxford Stamp Centre), Gill Kirkman (Borough of Eastbourne, Tourism, Leisure & Amenities), Keith Male (Bournemouth Tourism), Elaine Mellor (Weston-super-Mare Library), Morecambe Library, Richard Neale (Group Editor, *Hastings & St Leonards Observer*, *Bexhill on Sea Observer* and *Rye & Battle Observer*), Clare Newman (Science Museum, London), Paul Norris (Tourism Officer, Fylde Borough Council), Malcolm Orr-Ewing (publisher of *Signpost*), Penzance Library, Sharon Poole (North Somerset Museum Service), Saltdean Library, St Ives Library, Harry Thomas, Beth Thomson (Margate Library), Karen Trickey (Caradon District Council), Richard Turner (Publicity & Publications Manager, North Somerset Council), Pete Warrilow, Worthing Library.

While every effort has been made to trace people, the authors would also like to thank any others whose names have been inadvertently omitted and we apologize for any unintentional errors and misleading information that are subsequently discovered.

Introduction

The past is a foreign country: they do things differently there.[1]

But not *that* differently. The thing that impressed us most while doing the research for this book was not how different holidays in the inter-war years were from today, but how similar. It came as a surprise to learn, for example, that the bank holiday traffic jam was nothing new. Rows upon rows of vintage cars (of course they were not vintage then, but very ordinary) bumper to bumper, going nowhere, were a familiar sight on major routes into most of the big seaside towns from the thirties onwards. Sunbathing started in the twenties and that most important holiday fashion accessory, the pair of sunglasses, was common by the thirties.

There are differences of course. One man who found his Austin Seven boxed in by other parked cars along Bournemouth's Undercliff Drive simply picked it up by the back bumper and pulled it out into the road! The main differences are in style, taste and in technology. We do not now like swimming outdoors in the cold; in the twenties it was recommended, even in winter! No gentleman would today go on holiday wearing a striped blazer and no lady would think beach pyjamas and rubber bathing hats were the height of fashion. The aeroplane and the private car have replaced the train and the motor bus as the principal means of transport to the holiday destination. The main aim of the summer holiday, though, has not changed. As the *Official Guide to Hastings and St Leonards* explained in 1925:

> It is our pleasure when we take a holiday to give our moods and our tastes the rein. We feel free through our whole being even as we step from the train, and from the moment we leave the station we become truly ourselves and tastes which have had to be suppressed, and dreams which have been restricted to golden moments snatched from duty, are released. We are resolved to do as we please, and all we ask of the town we are visiting is that it shall have something for each inclination.[2]

[1] *The Go-between* by L.P. Hartley (Hamish Hamilton, 1953), copyright © 1953 by L.P. Hartley. This edition copyright © Douglas Brooks-Davies, 1997. Reproduced by permission of Penguin Books Ltd.
[2] *Official Guide to Hastings and St Leonards* for 1925. Reproduced by permission of Hastings Borough Council

The language is clearly from the period and you could read plane for train, but the meaning is timeless. We go on holiday to escape our daily routine. To 'give our moods and tastes the rein' – to do what we please, not what we have to do.

The annual holiday by the sea did not, of course, begin in the inter-war years. It can trace its roots as far back as 1626 when a lady called Mrs Farrow first discovered a spring at Scarborough. The popular habit of taking spa waters for medicinal purposes was then brought to the seaside. It was only a short step for the doctors of the day to recommend taking sea-water and sea-bathing. Drinking sea-water was thought, conveniently enough for the medical profession and the early boarding-house keepers, to cure gout. Bathing in the sea was a general pick-me-up. The first bathers were nude, and men and women bathed together. It took nineteenth-century prudery, combined with equally nineteenth-century commercialism, to introduce the bathing machine.

The inter-war years were the time when large numbers of people first enjoyed an annual holiday. Before the First World War, it was little more than a dream or a once-in-a-lifetime experience for many. It was, according to J.A.R. Pimlott, one of the first historians of the British seaside holiday, 'taken for granted as a luxury which could be enjoyed at a certain level of income, but which there was no special hardship in going without'[3]. By the end of the thirties, the annual holiday was the norm for 15 million people. The real breakthrough came in 1938 when the Holidays with Pay Act became law. All industrial workers were entitled to at least one week's paid holiday a year. Although this seems comprehensive, there were still some groups excluded from the legislation – farm workers, domestic servants and shop workers, for example.

It might then seem that only at the end the thirties were holidays enjoyed by people in large numbers. This was not the case. By the time the legislation came into force, many trades unions had negotiated private deals with employers for annual holidays. Many more could take unpaid leave. In the Lancashire cotton towns as early as the 1880s, workers were given a week off unpaid while the mill machinery was serviced. Most of them managed to go to the seaside in that week. In 1935, the authors of *The Survey of London Life and Labour* remarked that 'an annual summer holiday is today taken for granted by a large and increasing number of Londoners'[4]. Unfortunately there are few statistics to back up anecdotal evidence about numbers before 1938, but an impression is given of a gradual increase in the numbers taking holidays throughout the whole of the inter-war period.

The inter-war period was the time in which many of the basic elements of a modern lifestyle became a reality for the first time for significant numbers of people. Although the two decades are coloured by the Depression and unprecedented levels of unemployment, for many people the twenties and particularly the thirties gave them their first taste of affluence. This was a time of great contrasts. For millions of people working in what are known as the old staple industries of coal mining, shipbuilding, steel and cotton, it was a

[3] *The Englishman's Holiday* by J.A.R. Pimlott, Faber 1947.
[4] *A Social History of the Popular Seaside Holiday: Beside the Seaside* by James Walvin (Allen Lane, 1978), copyright © James Walvin, 1978. Reproduced by permission of Penguin Books Ltd.

time of great misery. The other side of the thirties coin, however, was the booming light manufacturing sector based around London and the Midlands. For those in secure jobs in the new industries of automobile manufacture, electricity and electrical goods and the service sector, life was becoming better. Against the backdrop of the Depression were the beginnings of prosperity, which was to come to full fruition only in the post-war years. Indeed, for those with the skills to work in the new industries, life was pretty good by pre-First World War standards. Much of what we now take for granted was available, for the first time, to those not exclusively drawn from the very wealthy in society.

Private car ownership increased dramatically. In 1914, there were only 140,000 motor vehicles of all types on the roads. By 1930, there were 1.5 million and by 1939, 3 million, 2 million of which were private cars. This was still only a fraction of the numbers of today, but it was a significant step in the right direction from the perspective of the ordinary traveller's freedom.

Home ownership showed an even more dramatic increase. Before the First World War even some of the most wealthy amongst the middle classes still rented homes. Property ownership was still concentrated in the hands of a tiny minority of wealthy landowners. Between 1920 and 1939, 2.5 million new homes were built for private sale and a further 1.5 million for council tenants. By the end of the thirties a basic semi-detached house could be bought for £450 – little more than double the price of a new car. With mortgage interest as low as 4.5%, it is not surprising that large numbers of people from the professions, the lower management grades and the skilled working classes took the opportunity to become homeowners. At no other time in our history was housing so affordable as in this the first housing boom, fifty years before the 1980s.

Most of the new houses would have been wired for electricity, but in 1920, only one in seventeen of all houses were. By 1930, it was one in three and by 1939 two in three. As well as lighting, electricity could be used to power a host of new consumer goods such as radios, gramophones, vacuum cleaners, washing machines and electric irons. Indeed, by the end of the thirties most of the electrical goods that we use today could be bought in some form. The television, though, was still only for the wealthy.

One of these new products, the radio, had far reaching effects on society itself. No longer were rural communities totally separate and insular. The latest news and sporting events such as the FA Cup Final or tennis from Wimbledon could be heard in even the most remote village. You did not even need to have electricity; a crystal set would do. Life in Britain had changed forever.

2 'Weston Suits Me!' from the Official Guide to Weston-super-Mare, 1939.

1 An Official Guide

Trying to decide what to do and where to go for a holiday this summer, we have found our thoughts turning unaccountably to prospects which astonish us. Perhaps it is heresy to say that we decidedly do not want to go to the same place and do the same things as last summer. Admittedly it was pleasant, but experience tells us that pleasant things seldom occur twice – and we say this in the face of a traditionalism which, in our country especially, keeps producing the same old pageants, the same old wireless programmes, the same old May Queens and the same old holiday trips year after year.[1]

Not surprisingly, it was quite common for many working-class holidaymakers to go to the same resort every year, often staying at the same boarding house. Those taking holidays for the first time were often influenced by friends and relatives in their choice of resort. Many went to the nearest big resort. Northerners went to Blackpool or Scarborough, Londoners to Margate, Southend or Brighton and Midlanders to Llandudno or to the East Coast. For many, of course, financial constraints played a big part in the decision, but this was often not the only reason. Nor was this pattern of holidaymaking limited only to the working classes. *Nash's Pall Mall Magazine* was aimed at a suburban, mainly female readership. Judging by its advertising material for motor cars and holidays abroad, its readers were quite well off, or at least aspired to be. Middle-class people also often followed the same well-worn path each year to a familiar resort. Many more chose to go and stay with relatives in the country every year.

In spite of these ingrained holiday patterns, many people followed the advice given by the Editor of *Nash's* and made a decision annually to choose a different holiday. For those with the resources as well as the will to make a choice, holiday resorts produced an annual official guide in which they set out their wares to prospective visitors. Often these brochures took the form of a prospectus for the town as whole, not just the features that would appeal to tourists. Many tried to entice people to come to the towns to live as well as to spend their holidays. Information was included on schools, libraries, rateable values, and electricity and gas. Those closest to the big cities often stressed the short commuting times to work that the new resident could swap for the smog of London, for example. Those furthest away made much of the delights of retirement there.

---

[1] Reprinted from *Nash's Pall Mall Magazine*, 1935, courtesy of The National Magazine Company.

These guidebooks were very much a statement not only of what was available to the visitor, but moreover how the town councillors would have liked the rest of the country to perceive their town. They provide a valuable insight, if not into what the towns were actually like, but at least into how the town councillors would have liked them to be seen.

A detailed study of this material reveals the features that must have been rated most highly in the minds of tourists in the twenties and thirties. It is quite surprising to learn that most seaside towns had an equable climate all year round. They were warm in winter and had plenty of sun in summer, although the heat was never oppressive. Invariably, there were shaded spots and the beaches were cooled by refreshing sea breezes. It did not matter whether it was Bournemouth or Blackpool; the climatic conditions were the same! Unlike today, when business is slack in the winter months, it was still common for those with sufficient leisure time to take extended breaks by the sea in winter, and most brochures stressed the favourable weather conditions compared with inland towns. Although by the end of the thirties sunbathing was almost a universal obsession amongst the young, it still seemed important not to suggest that seaside towns ever became too hot in the summer. This is probably a reflection on the conservatism of those responsible for producing the brochures, or possibly an attempt to retain the business of older visitors.

Another favoured theme was an interesting, historic past. Visits to ancient castles and monuments were very popular in the twenties and the thirties, probably even more so than today. It was then important to establish a resort's historical credentials. The author of Newquay's Guide for 1933 was extremely concerned that people might think the town was in any way 'new':

> The name of 'Newquay' has a very modern sound and gives the impression that it is a town of recent origin. But this is not really the case. In precisely the same way the name of New College, Oxford, conveys a similar impression to those who do not know that it is one of the oldest colleges in that University. When Newquay first took to itself its name it is now impossible to say, but as early as the year 1439 there are records which show that at that time Bishop Lacy of Exeter granted an indulgence for the construction, repair and maintenance of the little harbour. As the name Newquay is mentioned in Richard Carew's *Survey of Cornwall* published in the reign of Queen Elizabeth [I] it does not appear unreasonable to suppose that the name of the town dates back to 1439 – nearly 500 years.[2]

The striking thing about this passage is that it was given pride of place in the guide, the very first paragraph, before any mention of Newquay's beaches, climate or scenery. It seemed that every resort had some important historical connection, or some delightful old quarter completely unchanged from the days when the town was a tiny fishing village, or some ancient monument or battle site only a short walk or bus trip away. Nostalgia is nothing new.

---

[2] *Newquay on the Cornish Coast*, 1933, by permission of Newquay Tourism & Marketing Office.

One part of a historic past that always appealed was a link with smuggling. There was a romance associated with that time, which then was not too long past, when most of the resorts were little more than fishing villages and nearly everyone in the town from the squire and the clergy downwards aided and abetted in the illicit liquor game. Many guidebooks remind us that in quite recent times you could still find old fishermen who could tell tales of their town's smuggling past.

As well as the old, it was just as important to stress the new. The new swimming pool, cinemas, cafés and promenades were all given space in the brochure. It was also important to mention the modern facilities offered by the hotels and boarding houses. Although people wanted to go to see ancient relics, they did not want to stay in one!

Gardens were important and each resort had its own pleasure garden somehow just that little bit better than any other (**3, 4**). Sporting facilities would also be highlighted; many resorts had extensive facilities for swimming, golf, tennis, bowls, fishing and horse riding. The guidebooks would, of course, also extol the virtues of their town's summer and winter entertainment programmes. Many had orchestras playing throughout the year, not just for the summer season.

Most of these features would still be attractive to today's visitors, but if there is one thing that above all others distinguishes one period from another, it must be its view of the recent past. Resorts built on traditional lines with a row of hotels and shops directly opposite the seafront were considered unfashionable by the twenties. The authors of guides to resorts that were of later vintage and built differently were keen to mention this point. Bournemouth's Guide in 1926 tells us: 'Its seafront is not disfigured by rows of shops or terraces of houses .... Its numerous hotels and boarding houses and private residences lie half hidden amongst the pine trees and well-kept gardens'[3]. In the 1920 Bournemouth Guide they cocked a light-hearted snook at the fashions of the 1870s: 'The Winter Gardens Pavilion ... was the site of an archery ground, where ladies in crinolines and gentlemen in "peg top trousers" and with "Dundreary" whiskers shot at straw targets.'[4]

There is a definite distinction to be seen between the guidebooks of the more popular resorts of the day and those of resorts whose councils wished them to retain a degree of exclusivity. As we shall discuss later in this book, local councils often had to make a choice between appealing to the crowds or keeping the resort 'quiet'. It has to be remembered that this was a time when most British citizens took their holidays in this country. Comparatively few people could afford to go abroad. Consequently, the resorts often had more visitors than they could really cope with. Rather than appealing to all, there was a degree of what marketing consultants today would call 'brand differentiation'. The councils of the quieter resorts were keen to keep them quiet and not turn them into carbon copies of Blackpool or Margate. This passage from the *Official Guide to Eastbourne* for 1937 sums up the attitude well:

> From the point of view of the more 'popular' watering places Eastbourne has always seemed to possess a certain aloofness. For though she does not despise

[3] *Official Guide to Bournemouth* published 1926, by permission of Bournemouth Tourism.
[4] *Official Guide to Bournemouth* published 1920, by permission of Bournemouth Tourism.

3 Abbey Gardens at Torquay.

4 The Italian Gardens, Brighton. Each resort had its own pleasure gardens that were somehow just that little bit better than those at other resorts.

the day-tripper so heartily as she once did, when her citizens petitioned the railway company to discontinue cheap day returns from London, she holds out no particular allurements to him....

Yet still – and always likely to be – she is just a little bit aloof from the common throng of watering places that have taken the many-headed mob as their chief patron. This accounts for not the least of the attractions of Eastbourne, and there is in it less of the spirit of disdain for any one class of the community, than of happiness of contact with those that are responsive to the quiet, rational and enduring pleasures of life.[5]

The language used is clearly that of the period and the modern town of Eastbourne is certainly far removed from the image that this passage is likely to convey. Really though, all the author of this piece is saying is 'Don't come to Eastbourne expecting it to be like Blackpool,' or, more likely, Brighton. This kind of approach can be seen in official guides for other resorts. A guide to Torquay from the same period also indicated that pleasures appealing to the more loud and boisterous elements in the holidaying public could not be found at Torquay.

Although the features we have discussed were common to this type of guidebook throughout the period, there was a definite evolution in both the content of the material and the style of its presentation. This partly reflected a changing attitude among holidaymakers and partly a greater appreciation of the use of an image to sell a resort, rather than just the relaying of information.

Guidebooks of the early twenties were mostly small volumes with few illustrations. To today's eyes, they are unappealing and do not give a picture of happy holidaymakers having a good time. For the most part, they represented the rather outdated views of the town council about the purpose of a holiday and the type of visitors they expected to attract. Many still talked about 'health' rather than pleasure as being the main reason for visiting the seaside. It was quite common to quote death rate figures for the resort's elderly population, some even breaking this down into numbers dying from respiratory illnesses and other diseases! While it is true that most of the resorts owed their foundation to the era when 'taking the waters' to cure illness and restore health to the elderly and infirm was the main reason for a trip to the sea, times had, by the early twenties, moved on. Even well into the thirties it was not uncommon for the guidebooks to contain a chapter about the town's facilities for rest and recuperation.

A more light-hearted, unofficial twenties guide to Brighton underlines the shortcomings of many of the official guides:

As you know, these kinds of things [guidebooks] are noted for possessing two distinct features: *uninteresting* [italics as per original] and a *waste of money*. You

---

[5] *Eastbourne: Britain's favoured all-the-year-round resort Official Handbook 1937 Edition* by permission of the Borough of Eastbourne Tourism, Leisure & Amenities.

5 This guidebook to Hastings and St Leonards for 1933 used a particularly innovative design. (Hastings Borough Council)

will probably find that they were printed and published shortly after the old gentleman made his exit from the Ark.[6]

This is not quite true, as there was a new guide each year, but there was little difference in style between guidebooks published at the time this was written and those of twenty or even thirty years earlier. The good 'Doctor' then goes on to tell us that: 'quite a large number of [his] patients do not possess touring cars or pots of money.' This was another, probably deliberate, fault with these early guides. Most were written only with the wealthiest holidaymakers in mind.

By the end of the twenties the situation was beginning to improve. More colour was used, particularly on the covers of the brochures. Scenes featuring swimmers were popular. Often a different design was used each year. The Official Handbook to Eastbourne, from which the earlier quotation was taken, presents a particularly charming picture. There is a beach scene with group of happy bathers wearing colourful costumes in the foreground. In the background

[6] *Your visit to Dr Brighton* – an unofficial guidebook of the 1920s.

6 Guidebook to Lytham St Anne's, 1939. (Fylde Borough Council)

The Welfare of the People is the Highest Law

SALUS POPULI SUPREMA LEX

the very fine new bandstand (opened 1935) can be seen, and beyond that the pier (**colour plate 1**). The guide to Hastings and St Leonards for 1933 (**5**) shows a very innovative idea. There is a picture of the face of a clock. Inside the clock face is a picture of the pier. Two thirds of the clock face represents the hours of day and the remaining third the hours of night. The day-time image shows blue skies and the night-time image shows the pier in darkness lit up by electric light. The caption is 'Night and Day Bright and Gay' – after all, this is 1933!

By the end of the thirties, guides were much brighter and more inviting. Many more pictures were used and layouts were much improved. Most gave no doubt that their primary aim was to attract healthy summer visitors. In the more up-market resorts, there were still detailed sections on the benefits of a long winter stay or permanent residence, but for the most part, these were towards the back. Bournemouth's guide in 1939 (**7**) talked at length about the joys of spring, but this was more a reflection on the huge popularity of the town as a summer resort – by 1939 in the summer and on bank holidays it had more visitors than it could cope with. If some could be persuaded to take their holiday in spring, then all would be well and good.

Guidebooks provide the first glimpse of a twenties and thirties holiday, in the same way as they would have given the holidaymakers of the time their first impressions of next year's summer holiday on a wet afternoon in January.

The Bay, with Zig-zag Walk and
Undercliff Drive

7 An inside page of Bournemouth's 1939 guidebook showing the use of graphics to portray an image of quiet sophistication for the town. (Bournemouth Tourism)

2 Sun, Fun and Crowds

The names of Blackpool and Brighton are indelibly linked in people's minds with the idea of the classic summer holiday in England. Both were exceptionally popular in the inter-war period as holiday destinations.

By the end of the thirties, more than 7 million people visited Blackpool each year (**8**). Blackpool had been used to crowds and was well equipped to cater for them. As early as 1813, hordes of people from Preston and nearby industrial towns found their way, mostly on foot, to Blackpool for a 'dip in the briny'. What was only a few years earlier an exclusive resort for wealthy Lancashire and Yorkshire industrialists had already become public property. In the 1840s and 1850s, the railways brought still more people. For the most part these working people would have been trippers – staying only for the day and returning home in the evening. But it was the Wakes Weeks of the Lancashire mill towns that really made Blackpool as a resort. From about 1880, whole towns were shut down whilst the mill machinery was overhauled and the inhabitants decamped en masse to the seaside. More often than not, they went to Blackpool.

These early holidaymakers had only one week away from work throughout the whole year and were determined to make the most of it. They had saved up all year for this one week, when they could really enjoy themselves. Blackpool's entrepreneurs were equally determined to give them exactly what they wanted. The Winter Gardens were built in 1875 with the capacity for 6,000 people. Blackpool had not one but three piers, its trams and the famous tower all before the turn of the century. The Pleasure Beach evolved from a gypsy encampment in the early years of the twentieth century and by 1905 already had a helter-skelter and switchback rides (**9**).

So, as Blackpool entered the 'Roaring Twenties' it was already well equipped for the business of pleasure. Blackpool was and still is a rapidly changing place. A new and exciting attraction can quickly become old and boring to a change-hungry public. This was as true in the inter-war period as it is today. In 1928, Blackpool's Ferris Wheel, which had been built to rival the one at Coney Island, was dismantled. The trams were revamped twice in the period, looking very sleek and modern by the end of the thirties. The famous Blackpool Illuminations ran for most of the inter-war years (**colour plates 5 and 6**). They allowed the summer season to run on into autumn. The public's fascination with electric power ensured a spectacle capable of pulling in the crowds.

Blackpool's Pleasure Beach was completely redesigned in modern style by architect Joseph Emberton in the mid-thirties. The new attractions included the Great Dipper, the Grand National (**11**), the Ice Rink, the Fun House (**12**), the Indian Theatre, the Great Wheel, the Hall of Mirrors and the Water Caves. The Grand National was a double

8 Crowds on Blackpool's North Pier, c. 1920. This picture gives some idea of the amazing popularity of the resort.

9 Blackpool Pleasure Beach in the twenties before it was totally redesigned.

10 Blackpool entertainment in the twenties: the Big Dipper, c. 1922.

switchback ride with two cars that raced each other. The Fun House announced itself to visitors with a sign composed of rotating letters. Once inside, customers could enjoy, if that is the right word, a number of experiences. There was a giant slide with a drop of over thirty feet and a moving staircase. The staircase had two sections, each of which moved at different times. Perhaps the strangest of the attractions was a stage of moving barrels over which people walked. Whilst doing so they were subjected to an upward current of air, strong enough to raise the ladies' skirts. It must have been very funny for those watching their friends as seats were provided for spectators, but perhaps less so for those actually taking part! Other attractions included a crash bumper, a rocking floor, an ice walk, a drop floor, a shaking floor, shuffle boards and the 'Sahara Desert'.

At Blackpool you could have your fortune told by a gipsy, or by the thirties you could be 'radio-analysed' by a machine. You could buy oysters, whelks or jellied eels; sunglasses for fourpence; Blackpool rock or candy floss. You could see most of the famous stars of cinema and radio live at Blackpool's many theatres and pier pavilions. George Formby appeared at the Palace Theatre in 1921. Gracie Fields made *Sing As We Go* at Blackpool in 1934. Reg Dixon played the organ at the tower and at the Winter Gardens. You could see all the latest movies and dance the latest dances. Proprietors of Blackpool's entertainment palaces spared no expense to attract the big names. Blackpool even had its own version of the popular song *Doing the Lambeth Walk*.

However, Blackpool had its darker side. In the thirties, the Golden Mile (this is a misnomer as it is barely a quarter of a mile) probed new depths of depravity. It was host to numerous freak and peep shows. These included a man being crucified, the 'Tiny Man' and the 'Elephantine Woman'. A recurrent theme was starvation. Exhibits included

Blackpool's pleasure beach as revamped in the mid-thirties included the Fun House and the Grand National. The Grand National (11, left) was a double switchback ride on which the two cars raced together. The Fun House (12, below) contained all sorts of practical jokes, including a stage of moving barrels upon which participants were subjected to an upward blast of air, enough to raise the ladies' skirts, and a moving staircase of two halves which moved at different times. (Both pictures from the British Architectural Library, RIBA, London)

starving brides and honeymoon couples starving separated in a glass case. Usually payment was offered of several hundred pounds to couples to go without food for up to forty days. Rumour has it that most of the exhibits were a fraud and helped themselves to fish and chips as soon as the stalls closed each night. The pre-occupation with going without food is something difficult to appreciate today. Perhaps it is similar to the marathon dance competitions held at the time where the last couple left standing would win – the thirties could be a particularly cruel time. In spite of numerous attempts to close down these shows they remained a part of Blackpool's entertainment for most of the thirties.

Perhaps the most bizarre of all the exhibits was the ex-Rector of Stiffkey (pronounced Stewkey) in Norfolk, Harold Davidson (**13**). He became Rector of Stiffkey in 1906, but spent the majority of his time in London. He believed it was his calling to help fallen women. This earned him the title the 'Prostitutes' Padre'. A court in 1932 found that the help he was offering was more than spiritual and he was dismissed from his post. Davidson always protested his innocence. In an attempt to raise money for an appeal, or just in an attempt to raise money, he appeared on Blackpool's Golden Mile. He did not just appear, though. As part of Luke Gannon's show, he was exhibited starving in a barrel for fourteen days. For this, he was paid a fee of £500. On the first day of the exhibition, he drew crowds of 10,000 who each paid twopence to see the spectacle. Davidson made another appearance in Blackpool in 1935. This time he chose a glass cabinet and promised to fast until death unless his protestations were heard. The show was closed after ten days and Davidson was charged with attempted suicide. The case was dismissed after a doctor found him healthier after the fast than before it. Davidson continued his career as a showman. Finally, he appeared at Skegness in 1937, giving a lecture to a caged lion – from inside the cage. The lion killed him. He was buried at his original parish church in Stiffkey.

There was certainly plenty to see and do at Blackpool, but the one thing you could not have though was peace and quiet. Working people liked crowds. They lived in crowded towns and cities and worked in crowded factories. They enjoyed the noise and bustle of a big resort – or so it was assumed.

In 1939, a Mass Observation report was published in *Picture Post,* which shows that this assumption was not true. A survey was conducted in a 'typical', but unspecified, inland industrial town about attitudes towards holidays. They found that the majority of people wanted to go away for their holidays and 85 per cent of those interviewed actually did. Out of those interviewed, a significant number expressed a desire to go to a quiet resort. Very few actually did. Many of those wanting to go to a quiet resort actually went to Blackpool. One holidaymaker who talked to *Picture Post* said:

> How I spend my holidays and how I want to spend my holidays are two different things. I should like to be carried away to some secluded spot where work and crowds are things unheard of. I shall be carried away to Blackpool.[1]

[1] From the article 'So This is Blackpool' by Tom Harrison, in *Picture Post*, 1 July 1939. Reproduced courtesy of IPC Magazines Ltd.

13 The darker side of Blackpool's entertainment: people queue to see the ex-Rector of Stiffkey, Harold Davidson, in a barrel, September 1932. (Popperfoto)

The reason for the popularity of Blackpool was simply one of value for money. Blackpool was well organized. It offered quality entertainment, in fact some of the best available anywhere outside London, and was able to do this at a price working people could afford. Quieter resorts were more expensive and difficult to get to. Most working people compromised and chose Blackpool.

Brighton, like Blackpool, was popular. It was within easy reach of London, being for most Londoners only an hour away by train. It was quicker to reach from central London than some of the London suburbs. Graham Greene in *Brighton Rock* paints a wonderful picture of hundreds, if not thousands, of Londoners descending upon Brighton on the May Bank Holiday using every means of motorized transport imaginable. Graham Greene also shows us another side to Brighton: that of the race gangs and violence. Brighton always had a slightly raffish reputation; it had the Prince Regent to thank for that. After the First World War, a certain seedy atmosphere prevailed. Brighton did well out of the war. Many rich and leisured people whose holidays abroad were curtailed came to Brighton instead. Brighton was home to convalescent soldiers and attracted its share of displaced persons seeking shelter from the occasional Zeppelin raids on London. Tales abounded of high rents and profiteering and of how families were displaced from their lodgings while their men were fighting for King and Country to make room for more lucrative lets to foreign refugees. Brighton's wartime prosperity attracted all sorts of undesirable and criminal elements shortly after the war. It was just the kind of atmosphere for gangs such as Pinky's (the anti-hero in *Brighton Rock*) to flourish. If you believe Harold Clunn, author of *Famous South Coast Pleasure Resorts – Past and Present,* the reign of the gangs was brought to an end by the end of the twenties. If you believe Graham Greene, it lasted well into the thirties.

Nevertheless, Brighton had a somewhat racy reputation that was not present in Blackpool. Its proximity to London made it popular for the 'bright young things' from the city to slip away by car to Brighton for a weekend in one of the 'posh' hotels. Even in 1939, Antonia White writing for *Picture Post* felt there was something special about going to Brighton:

> If one man says to another 'I'm off to Brighton for the week-end,' the same knowing look comes back in the other's eyes as if he had said 'I'm off to Paris.' .... There's still a feeling that there's something delightfully dashing about going to *Brighton* [her italics].[2]

Brighton did, in many respects, manage to be all things to all people. Certainly, Brighton had its share of gin palaces, whelk stalls, fish and chip shops, donkey rides and 'kiss-me-quick' hats, but it also had its upmarket hotels. *Picture Post* identified two main types of visitor to Brighton:

[2] From the article 'Brighton' by Antonia White, in *Picture Post*, 12 August 1939. Reproduced courtesy of IPC Magazines Ltd.

There were the August Bank Holidaymakers who packed the beach like brightly-coloured sardines, for whom 'Brighton' meant the piers, the cafés, the dance halls and the winkle stalls. And there was an entirely different 'holiday population' who avoided Brighton in the height of summer and came for long stays in the spring and autumn. They were mainly 'country people' who preferred the solid English comfort of Brighton to the unknown 'horrors' of 'abroad', as well as the stockbrokers, chorus girls and racing men who dashed down from London for the week-end.[3]

Among the out-of-season visitors was the Conservative Prime Minister, Andrew Bonar Law, and many other politicians of the time.

Bournemouth, like Brighton, managed to get this tricky balance right (**14, 15**). In the late thirties, Bournemouth was inundated with day-trippers on bank holidays. According to the local newspapers of the time, there was an uneasy truce between the locals and the trippers. The *Bournemouth Times* in August 1938 comments on the previous Bank Holiday Monday (in those days the August Bank Holiday was always the first Monday in August, not the last) in an article headed:

BOURNEMOUTH'S AUGUST BANK HOLIDAY SCANDAL
Day-Trippers' Paradise On Undercliff Drive
What was wrong with Bournemouth on Bank Holiday? There was plenty of sun, a gentle breeze and a record crowd of people, but the sea front was not quite the delightful place visitors used to know a few years ago.[4]

Traffic congestion is cited as the main cause but the reporter still sees fit to mention that:

Groups of youths, some wearing gaudy paper hats with inscriptions such as 'Come up and see me sometime' parading along the Drive singing the latest dance hits was a sight which would have shocked most Bournemouth visitors not so many years ago.

Yes, Bournemouth has certainly changed and if August Bank Holiday 1938 was anything to go by a good many residents must have emphatically decided that change has not been for the better.[4]

The Bournemouth of ten years earlier was a very quiet place indeed, judging by a comparison between Bournemouth and the Lido (Venice Lido) drawn by Sir Percival Phillips in the *Daily Mail*. He described Bournemouth in terms of the very essence of domestic bliss: families enjoying quiet picnics from the beach bungalows along the front, old gentlemen taking the occasional dip in the sea. No sign of any day-trippers or indeed any of the sophisticated crowds that populated the Lido at that time.

[3] 'Brighton', *Picture Post*, 12 August 1939. Reproduced courtesy of IPC Magazines Ltd.

[4] From an article in the *Bournemouth Times*, August 1938, by permission of the *Bournemouth Advertiser*.

The Square, Bournemouth, showing Bobby's department store (14, above), and Branksome Chine, also at Bournemouth (15, below). Bournemouth was a quiet resort that was nevertheless extremely popular during the inter-war years.

Bournemouth had always been a sedate resort. In the nineteenth century, its councillors fought a rear-guard action against the railways for fear that an influx of plebeian visitors might put off the wealthy invalids that patronized the town. In so doing, they almost killed off Bournemouth as a resort. In the thirties they forbade whelk stalls on the sea front and slot machines on the pier were banned well into the sixties.

Although Bournemouth was far from racy, it was certainly successful. By the end of the thirties its official guide had reached the state of being a hardback book absolutely bursting with advertisements for first-class hotels. The *AA Hotel Handbook of 1938* listed no fewer than 120 appointed hotels in Bournemouth, five of them receiving the organization's highest five-star classification. That is nearly 50 per cent more than any other seaside town. Torquay was the nearest rival, boasting eighty-three appointed hotels. Brighton had only twenty-seven. Furthermore, in the standard handbook members visiting Bournemouth were encouraged to get the *Hotel Handbook*, as there was insufficient space to include all the hotels recommended to members in Bournemouth.

If, like the gentleman interviewed during a Mass Observation (as mentioned earlier in this chapter), you wanted to escape the crowds, but unlike him, you had the resources to do it where would you have gone? Many of the loud and brash resorts of the twenties and thirties had quiet middle-class neighbours. Blackpool had St Anne's, Brighton had Hove and Margate had Broadstairs. These smaller towns seemed to exist quite happily next to their larger sisters without trouble in the inter-war years and continue to do so today. Most tried to maintain their exclusivity by promoting the more genteel side of their character. The authors of the guide to St Anne's, for example, stressed golf and riding as being the most popular of its holiday sports. Frinton in Essex actually banned coach parties.

Blackpool was exceptionally good at catering for the holidaying public en masse. Brighton managed somehow to juggle the needs of the 'bright young things' from London, the day-trippers and the older, more staid, wealthy visitors. Bournemouth was staid, but still managed to attract the crowds. The smaller, middle-class resorts found their own niche in the holiday market. But what of the resorts that did not quite fit into either group? Morecambe was not quite Blackpool, nor was it St Anne's. Weston-super-Mare had been described as the 'Blackpool of the West', but still saw itself primarily as a health resort catering for the wealthy invalid.

Hastings was a case in point. Hastings was not Brighton, nor was it Hove or Eastbourne. The agonizing dilemma for the local council was which way to go: appeal to the crowds and bring in more money at the risk of losing the resort's traditional customers who would be put off by the noise and bustle the trippers would bring, or retain the traditional visitors looking for peace and quiet and somehow keep the hordes out? There was heated debate in the council chamber and the local press. The results were usually an uneasy compromise that never quite worked. In the inter-war period, there was so much money around for the holiday business that it hardly mattered. Problems were to come much later.

3 The Remote and Unspoilt

There has long been a desire in our culture to escape from the modern way of life and go back to an older and simpler time. The Georgians looked back to the Classical era and the Victorians romanticized the Middle Ages. In the machine age of the twentieth century there was always a feeling that progress had somehow been too fast. Some of the innocence of the past had been lost. Even in the twenties and thirties there was a feeling that modern life had become too commercial and was somehow not real in the same way that the past was. It is no coincidence that the most popular style of family home in the inter-war period was mock Tudor.

On holiday, there was a great desire among large parts of the population to escape modern life. These people were the new middle classes – the teachers, civil servants and junior professionals. They were the new suburbanites that bought semi-detached houses by the million and the first motor cars that were genuinely available to the public at a reasonable cost. They were not looking for the brash commercialism of Blackpool or even the sophistication of the South of France. They wanted to rediscover the real, the unspoilt and the romantic.

Cornwall had a lot to offer; it was remote. As recently as 1810, Cornwall was only accessible from the rest of Britain by packhorse. Even in 1901, the census only listed one Cornish resort as a watering place – Newquay, with a population of 3,000. In the thirties, Cornwall was still remote, and you could not get more remote than Land's End (**16**). Take this passage from the *Official Guide to Land's End Country* for 1933:

> The lack of penetration by railways undoubtedly enabled the district to preserve its character as a remote and secluded area, although its inhabitants have always been a self-contained and a wonderfully self-reliant community. Until the advent of motor transport, the visitor was in the presence of all the conditions of a pre-railway era, and despite a great increase in motoring these conditions have not entirely been displaced.[1]

Cornwall was remote most of all from the trippers. The fast Cornish Riviera Express from Paddington did the 281 miles to Newquay in $6\frac{1}{4}$ hours in 1933 and cost £5 16s 4d first class and £3 9s 10d[2] third class for a return ticket. By 1939, ticket prices had

---

[1] *The Land's End Country Official Guide* published in 1933, by permission of Penwith District Council.
[2] *Newquay on the Cornish Coast*, 1933, by permission of Newquay Tourism & Marketing Office.

16 *You could not get more remote than Land's End. Until the arrival of the motor car, you could only have reached it by foot or on a horse. Land's End was presented as belonging to the pre-railway era.*

dropped to £3 13s 8d and £2 9s 1d[3] respectively. These prices would hardly have been within reach of the typical working-class holidaymaker who spent no more than £10 on his entire holiday, for himself and his wife and children.

There is some evidence that by the end of the thirties the nature of visitors to Cornwall was changing. In 1938, Mr G.O. Redfearn gave talks in both Penzance and St Ives about the reduction in spending power of visitors to Cornwall. It would appear that more visitors were staying at boarding-houses, farmhouses and at campsites than at the larger hotels. Many of the visitors were, however, arriving by car so would hardly have been working class. It was just that the very wealthy former visitors to the Duchy were now going abroad.

As well as remote, Cornwall was romantic. Ever since the first visitors came to the sea there has been a fascination with its power and majesty. In Victorian times crowds often flocked to Blackpool when stormy weather was predicted to see the spectacle. A classic series of early twentieth-century postcards was produced showing huge waves striking promenades and coastal defences with such force that the spray dwarfs the hotels along the front (**colour plate 7**). The sea was untamed nature. It could be beautiful; it could also be dangerous. The sea at rough and rugged Cornwall carried an extra fascination. Bathing was hazardous at high tide from some Cornish beaches. There were tales of storms and shipwrecks.

S.P.B. Mais, author of many guidebooks of the period to Devon and Cornwall, sums up the allure of the Cornish sea:

> Nowhere else does the sea make its terrific power felt so strongly. It may be friendly and full of colour to us in the summer, but the churchyards are full of bodies of shipwrecked sailors, masts still emerge from the water at low tide, and skeletons of old ships stand out from the wind-blown sands.
>
> The grave faces of the fishermen, to us so dignified and picturesque, owe their lives to the Atlantic. When we are not here a relentless war is being waged by the men whose living depends on what they draw out of the sea, and whose lives depend on themselves not being drawn into it. The sea in Cornwall is ever present. We cannot, if we would, withdraw ourselves from its restless song, that eerie melody at once so soothing and so tragic. The power of the waves during a storm, as they thunder against these granite cliffs, holds us spellbound and makes us wonder more than a little at the fineness of man's spirit who seeks to harness even the monster to secure his ends.[4]

Those who plied their trade on the ocean were held in high regard by the holidaymaking public. Cornish fishermen were especially revered. Their lives were thought to be simple and uncomplicated, unchanged for centuries. They were of a different ilk to us, dignified and remote. As early as the 1880s the Newlyn School, a group of artists, specialized in

---

[3] *Guide to North Cornwall, Newquay, Perranporth, Tintagel, Padstow, Bude etc* published by Ward Lock & Co. Ltd in 1939.
[4] *The Cornish Riviera* by S.P.B. Mais, published in 1928 by the Great Western Railway Company.

17 The Warren, Polperro. It is easy to see how the smugglers of times past hid themselves away in this maze of tiny streets. (Photograph taken by A.E. Raddy; courtesy of Rex Raddy)

painting Cornish fishermen and their families. In the twenties, postcards depicting them and their boats were popular (**colour plate 8**).

As in many other seaside towns the authors of guidebooks to Cornish resorts were at pains to point out their town's connection with the smuggling trade. Polperro (**17**), for example, 'is a maze of miniature streets, alleys, steep steps and ancient courts that are honey-combed with secret exits, cupboards, cellars and other passages by which, in olden days, the Revenue officers were eluded and the bold smugglers, almost jovially friendly in their defiance, were able to avoid pursuit while saving their contraband cargoes.'[5] Newquay, we are told, was policed in 1775 by a Revenue officer who was prepared to turn a blind eye to the smugglers.

The romance of Cornwall did not just come from its present or comparatively recent past. It was a land of mystery, myth and legend. The legend of King Arthur was almost made for Cornwall's tourist trade. The story is that Uther Pendragon fought Gorlois, Duke of Cornwall, at Damelioc, a few miles from Wadebridge. Uther was victorious and he stole Gorlois' wife Igraine. She gave birth to Uther's child who was to become King Arthur. King Arthur reputedly met his death at Slaughter Bridge near Camelford in AD 542 in his final battle with Mordred. It is possible that Camelford may have been Camelot. The mystery surrounding Arthur's life makes the story all the more fascinating and these sites all the more worth visiting. Already his castle at Tintagel was a Mecca for visitors, and guidebooks warned of crowds.

As well as its past, Cornwall had its present. Its beaches were perfect for sunbathing (**colour plate 9**). Nowhere else was the sun so strong or the skies so clear. Its climate was ideal. All the guidebooks told us it was warmer in Cornwall in winter than in most Mediterranean resorts. You could even swim in the sea in winter. A Great Western Railway poster produced in 1923 showed photographs of Miss Eileen Nolan and her sister Peggy bathing at St Agnes in February. The photographs were also printed in the *Daily Mirror.* The *Railway Gazette* would have us believe it was not just a publicity stunt. We have our doubts though!

In summer, Cornwall was ideal for swimming and the new sport of 'surf riding'. Surfing had not yet entered the English language, but people did it at Newquay in the thirties (**colour plate 10**) – thirty years before the Beach Boys and *Surfin' USA*!

[5] *Looe and District 1939 Official Guide,* published by the Looe Urban District Council, by permission of Caradon District Council.

4 Travelling in Style

For most people, the holiday itself began with a train journey. The trip by train was all part of the adventure of going away. How exciting it must have been for children travelling by train to get the first glimpse of the sea as the train neared its destination. The film *Bank Holiday* (1938), starring Margaret Lockwood, started with a train journey. It is a bank holiday weekend and the station is absolutely packed with holidaymakers. It is a chaotic scene. Arthur (Wally Patch) and his wife May (Kathleen Harrison) are taking their children away for the holiday. They are carrying suitcases, fishing nets and buckets and spades. The children are excited and play up. On the same train is Doreen (Rene Ray) who is hoping to enter a beauty contest. She has her rather dowdy friend Milly (Merle Tottenham) with her. A young courting couple, Geoffrey (Hugh Williams) and Catherine (Margaret Lockwood) are going away for the weekend. They plan to pretend that they are married and stay at the Grand Hotel. An announcement is broadcast saying that the train for 'Bexborough' is leaving from another platform. There is panic as people rush to change platforms. It is difficult to find a seat on the train. Finally, in a cloud of steam the train pulls away.

Most trains were pulled by a steam locomotive, but by the thirties the journey could be made in the swift silence of the most modern electric trains. In 1934, the *Brighton Belle* was brought into service by the Southern Railway, hauling an all-Pullman electric luxury express from London to Brighton. This service, together with the *Bournemouth Belle*, initially hauled by steam, continued well into the post-war era. The *Brighton Belle* ran up to 1972.

Rail travel and holiday resorts were inextricably linked for many years. In many cases, the railways, being a convenient means of transporting large numbers of people, actually launched towns that were no more than fishing villages as major holiday destinations. The railway companies themselves did a great deal to publicize holiday resorts and attract customers both for the resorts and, given that most holidaymakers went by train, for their own services. Their principal means of attracting customers was through posters placed at the stations from which people commuted to work and on the trains themselves. These posters were often subsidized by the local councils of the resorts, such was the co-operation between the resorts and the railways. Since the railway companies operated in different areas of the country, it was in their interests for holidaymakers to visit specific areas of the British coastline. The LNER promoted the East Coast as the 'drier side', the Southern Railway the 'sunny South', Great Western pushed 'Glorious Devon' and the 'Cornish Riviera' and the LMS concentrated on the north-west coast – Blackpool, Morecambe and North Wales (**colour plate 12**).

SEE THE BEAUTY OF THE WEST FROM A *"Bristol"* COACH

Regular daily Bus Services and Coach Tours serve all the beauty spots, seaside resorts and places of interest in the West Country. Programme of Coach Tours and Timetable of Bus Services will be sent post free to any address on request.

All Bus Services and Coach Tours start from BEACH GARAGE AND BUS STATION (on Sea Front). This is also the Booking Office and Starting Point for Express Coach Services to all parts of the Country; and Booking Office for all Air Services from Weston-super-Mare.

PRIVATE OUTINGS

SALOON BUSES
AND COACHES
ARE ALWAYS
AVAILABLE FOR
PRIVATE HIRE
BY PARTIES

Address all Road and Air Travel enquiries to:—

BRISTOL TRAMWAYS & CARRIAGE CO., LTD.
BEACH GARAGE AND BUS STATION, WESTON-SUPER-MARE
Telephone 110

Chief Offices at Bristol. Other Branches at Bath, Cheltenham, Coleford. Gloucester, Highbridge, Swindon, Wells, and Wotton-under-Edge.

BEACH GARAGE. Accommodation for 600 Private Cars. Open day and night. Official Repairers to R.A.C.

Beach Garage and Bus Station—starting point of all bus and coach services—deals with 2,000,000 passengers annually

18 *The railways did not have it all their own way. The motor bus was already making its presence felt, either for excursions from the resort (as this advertisement from the Weston-super-Mare Guide for 1939 shows) or for cheap travel to the seaside itself. Note the streamlined style of the vehicle. (North Somerset Council)*

The inter-war period was the golden age of the railway poster. Designs were of high quality and great visual appeal. The poster artists were adept at creating appropriate and distinctive images for the areas of the coastline that they were advertising. Those employed by the LNER were particularly skilled in this art. Tom Purvis' 'East Coast by LNER' campaign in the late twenties (**colour plate 11**) showed youthful bathers in modern costumes painted in abstract style. Scarborough was portrayed as sophisticated by W. Smithson Broadhead – showing a smart middle-aged couple in front of a view of the coastline. Skegness, by contrast, was presented as the place to have unsophisticated fun, through the long-running 'Jolly Fisherman' campaign, which began in 1908, by the Great Northern Railway.

As well as posters, the railway companies produced literature advertising the resorts. Great Western published volumes on their gem resorts in 'Glorious Devon' and the 'Cornish Riviera' and a series called *Holiday Haunts* and Southern Railway published *Hints for Holidays* every year.

In spite of the popularity of the railways and their poster campaigns, rail travel as the principal form of transport was already under threat from the road. At the lower end of the market, motor buses (**18**) competed on price and at the top end, the private car was already making inroads into the railway business.

The motor bus was not only cheap, but could be more flexible, with the ability to pick passengers almost from their doorstep and deliver them direct to their destination. The bus gave rise to works' social club and pub-organized outings to the sea (**19**). Buses allowed the people to travel to their destinations together, holiday together and travel back

19 Pub, social club and works outings were a popular feature of coach travel in the inter-war years. This group is the Alligator Leather Goods works outing to Clacton in 1935. (Julia Braggs)

together. These working-class holidaymakers, often the first of their families to enjoy an annual holiday, looked for familiarity in the form of familiar faces in the alien surroundings of the holiday resorts. For many working-class holidaymakers, the bus or charabanc trip to the coast was their only experience of holidays. According to J. Walvin in *Beside the Seaside* (1978):

> There is something particularly cohesive about trips in a motor coach which is absent in a train.... Coach trips evolved their own games, their songs, their customs: the first child to catch sight of the sea – or Blackpool Tower – would win a sweet or a chocolate.[1]

A more serious long-term threat to the railways was the private car, although at the time, their presence made little dent in the railway trade. The motoring organizations, the AA and the RAC, were already producing their well-known handbooks packed with details of hotel accommodation and other useful advice. By the thirties, certain holiday routes had already passed into motoring legend as a contemporary RAC tour of Devon and Cornwall points out:

> A warning is necessary in the case of the roads into and through the North Devon Coast district, particularly Porlock Hill. A newcomer or beginner should not fall into the error of regarding the ascent as simple, just because he sees others make light of it with the same make of car as his own. Porlock Hill definitely demands an efficient driver and a car in good fettle. At holiday times, or on a busy day, the novice had better take the toll road.[2]

Many motorists, even today, have felt the sense of achievement on a successful climb or descent of Porlock Hill or have noted the pitfalls of those whose driving or machine failed them.

The car brought a new style of holiday, the touring holiday, where the motorist would travel along the coast stopping at several seaside towns rather than staying at just one for the whole week or fortnight. Once at the resort, the motorist was not, of course, constrained to remain in one place, whether touring or not; he could use his hotel as a base to explore the surrounding countryside. Morecambe was a favourite choice from which to explore the Lake District. Whitby, Scarborough and Bridlington were similarly used as handy access to Whitby Moors, Forge Valley and East Yorkshire, while Llandudno, Colwyn Bay and Rhyl were conveniently located for the valleys and mountains of Wales. This type of holiday was later to become the norm for many holidaymakers, but in the thirties, these motorists were pioneers. Already they were regarded with suspicion by those fortunate enough to live in the countryside and have the leisure time to enjoy it.

---

[1] *A Social History of the Popular Seaside Holiday: Beside the Seaside* by James Walvin (Allen Lane, 1978), copyright © James Walvin, 1978. Reproduced by permission of Penguin Books Ltd.
[2] *The RAC Tour around Devon & Cornwall*, 1930s, by permission of the Royal Automobile Club.

NOW YOU CAN AFFORD
BIGGER CAR MOTORING

DEEP, luxurious comfort that soothes you into happy forgetfulness of business worries — smooth power, joyously exhilarating or pleasantly docile to your merest whim. Extra roominess and comfort, a still finer degree of controllability—*plus* the road-holding and extra wide margin of safety that only Bigger car motoring can give. *That* is motoring interpreted by the Vauxhall Big Six. It seems incredible that such luxury should be obtainable for less than £500.

Yet for as little as £325—and an annual tax of only £15—you can own a fine, roomy 5-seater saloon built in true Vauxhall tradition. This is a car whose qualities make it as though built to order—a car you can be proud of possessing. And being a Vauxhall, it has such features as entirely automatic chassis lubrication, synchro-mesh gears, pedomatic starting and no-draught ventilation, while its modern streamlined coachwork—distinctive but not blatant—dominates the road and compels attention in any gathering of better-class cars.

There are two chassis types of Vauxhall Big Six. The Standard chassis with a 20-h.p. or 27-h.p. engine for five-seater coachwork. The Regent chassis (with 19 in. extra wheelbase, larger tyres with two spares, etc., 27-h.p. engine only) for seven-seater and specially roomy coachwork.

But 20 minutes at the wheel will tell you more than we could ever hope to—and a word with your local dealer will secure this.

VAUXHALL BIG SIX

Standard Chassis (20 h.p. or 27 h.p.). Saloon with No-Draught Ventilation, £325. Wingham Convertible Cabriolet, £395. Tickford Foursome Drophead Coupé, £365. Regent Chassis (27 h.p., 10 ft. 10 ins. wheelbase). Grosvenor 7-seater Limousine, £550. Newmarket 5-6 seater sports Saloon, £550. Continental Touring Saloon, £590. Catalogues on request from Vauxhall Motors Ltd., Luton, Beds.

20 The motorist at play. The seaside was a common feature in advertisements for private cars. (Vauxhall Motors)

Motoring opened up many remote towns and villages in Devon and newly popular Cornwall to a limited number of holidaymakers. The car allowed the middle classes to seek quieter holidays away from seaside towns that were becoming increasingly popular with the working classes.

Another variation on the early motoring holiday was caravanning. Caravan holidays in the thirties were by no means as well catered for as in the present age. Caravan parks were not to arrive until the sixties. Motorists would make private arrangements with local farmers to park their caravan on their land for a few nights. Usually they would be able to stock up with farm-grown provisions at the same time. A caravan holiday in those days was suited to those who sought peace and quiet on their vacation and given that car ownership was a pre-requisite, was exclusively middle class.

Styling of caravans in the twenties was similar to that of contemporary cars, rather upright and 'boxy'. In the thirties, more rounded, streamlined forms were introduced (**colour plate 13**), again reflecting contemporary tastes in automotive styling. Streamlining of caravans had certain practical advantages in reducing wind resistance and making the caravan less of a burden for the towing car, but its main function was to emphasise modernity. In many designs, a two-tone colour combination was used which went well with similar paint schemes used on the cars of the era.

Although the caravan when towed by a car was designed to express modernity, when standing still, it became a temporary home. As such, owners wanted a degree of homeliness. Paradoxically, as it may appear, this homeliness was often represented by Tudor style stained glass windows similar to those seen on the new semi-detached houses. Some designs even had leaded lights. The middle classes too needed familiarity in unfamiliar surroundings.

LNER had its own answer to the caravan market when it introduced camping coaches in 1933 (**colour plate 14**). For a fee of £2 10s, six people could share a coach equipped with linen, cooking utensils and crockery for a week. These coaches were usually located in sidings near stations. In spite of their similarity to caravanning, they probably competed more with holiday camps for potential customers. This form of holiday was evidently popular, as GWR and LMS soon followed the LNER example.

Many enterprising individuals were also offering this kind of holiday on a much smaller scale. In the village of Farmoor, near Oxford, for example, a local garage proprietor took people on holiday to Hayling Island in Hampshire by car. Once there, people stayed in a variety of accommodation, including an old bus converted for the purpose (**21**).

As well as the private car, the motorcycle sold in large numbers in the inter-war period. In combination with a sidecar, it was particularly good for touring. Famous names such as Ariel, BSA and Triumph were already on the roads. This form of transport provided the freedom of the car on a smaller budget, although long distances must have been uncomfortable.

With relatively few cars on the road, the motorist was pampered by today's standards. Many hotels provided garages, some even had chauffeurs and mechanics on the premises (see Chapter 10). One feature of thirties motoring was the roadhouse, which was a large public house or hotel offering alcoholic refreshment and accommodation for motorists. Roadhouses had extensive facilities including garaging, petrol stations, cocktail bars,

21 As well as railway carriages, old buses could be used as holiday accommodation. This group is on Hayling Island in 1934. (Francis Harris)

restaurants, ballrooms and swimming pools. The swimming pools were often floodlit and used in the evenings.

The drawbacks of motoring, however, were already starting to appear. The problem of congestion was serious in the thirties. Many resorts in the summer season were packed with traffic, both cars and buses, and the annual holiday traffic jam was already an inevitable part of the trip to and from the holiday resort.

The most modern form of transport was, of course, the aeroplane (**22**). Flying was considered new and exciting in the thirties and as such provided a form of entertainment to holidaymakers. A thirties *Ward Lock Guide to Brighton* explains the delights of Shoreham Airport:

> The Airport is thoroughly well equipped and provides a very popular excursion from Brighton. Guides are available to conduct visitors around the hangars to explain the various operations connected with landing and taking off, etc., and 'joyrides' [**23**] can be had at very low charge.[3]

The airport building itself opened on 13 June 1936 and was very modern in style. It was constructed of white concrete, with the classic thirties feature of curved wrap-round

[3] *A Pictorial and Descriptive Guide to Brighton and Hove,* late 1930s, published by Ward, Lock & Co. Ltd.

22 Air travel was new and exciting in the inter-war period. Many local aerodromes offered short 'joy rides' to holidaymakers. This is Shoreham Airport, built in 1936. (Steven Braggs)

23 These are the kind of planes that would have been used for 'joy rides'; these are based in Bournemouth. Julia Braggs remembers flying to the Isle of Wight in one of these aircraft from an aerodrome near Bournemouth. (Julia Braggs)

windows with horizontal glazing bars. The whole structure was dominated by a central control tower with a modernist clock face without numbers, just dashes, below the highest window. Shoreham Airport today is often used as an airport location for television films set in the period.

At the opposite end of the scale to the new aeroplanes was one of the earliest forms of holiday travel – the steamer. Steamers predated the railways as a means of transporting large numbers of people to holiday resorts. The resort of Margate had a long association with this form of transport.

Margate's history as a resort goes back as far as 1736 when the first sea bathers came there. By 1800, around 18,000 Londoners were visiting Margate. They travelled by hoy, which was a single-masted sailing boat of between 60 and 80 tons. The trip could take anything from eight hours to three days depending on the state of the tides and the weather conditions. The steamers took over from the hoys. By the 1830s, around 100,000 people were making the same journey by steamer.

In spite of the arrival of the railway in Margate in 1846, travel by steamer continued to be popular. Indeed, this form of transport continued to flourish well into the twentieth century. In the mid-twenties, three new steamers plied the trade from London to Margate: the *Eagle*, the *Golden Eagle* and the *Crested Eagle*. In the thirties the *Queen of the Channel* and the *Royal Daffodil* were launched to serve the same route.

The London to Margate steamers gave loyal service in 1940 when they were used to ferry stricken soldiers back from the beaches of Dunkirk. After the war, they resumed their original role and continued to take holidaymakers to Margate right up to 1967.

Before leaving this chapter, it is worth mentioning the seaside tram. Before 1914 many resorts had put in tramlines, but in the twenties and thirties the situation was different. The tram had acquired unpleasant associations with crowded and often dirty inner city areas. A reputation as a safety hazard to cyclists, who often got their bicycle wheels stuck in the tramlines, did not help. Many resorts ripped up tramways as part of modernization programmes and the tram was destined to be yesterday's transport. Blackpool was almost alone in improving and updating its tramway. Blackpool's tramlines were always separate from the road, thus avoiding any potential danger to cyclists and motor vehicles. They were, and are still, very much a part of a holiday in Blackpool.

In the years that followed the Second World War, the new forms of transport, the bus, the private car and the aeroplane, were to grow in importance as a means of getting to the holiday destination. In particular, the growth in the use of the car allowed many more holidaymakers to explore the remoter resorts of Devon, Cornwall and Scotland. Camping and caravanning were to explode in popularity in the sixties and seventies, not as a means for the middle-classes to escape the crowds, but to allow people to go to the destination of their choice at a price acceptable to nearly everyone. The aeroplane, however, was to begin the decline of the Great British holiday when millions of people were given the chance to experience the guaranteed sun of the continental resorts.

5 Sartorial Elegance

The seaside holiday was a marvellous opportunity for dressing up, especially for the young. Holidaymakers could leave behind their drab office suits or factory overalls and go to the sea looking like movie stars. The holiday atmosphere was first rate for attracting a potential partner and a stroll along the esplanade was the ideal place to show off the latest thing in daywear fashions.

The latest fashion in the twenties for women was the boyish look. Dresses hung straight down from the shoulders, with no waist, forming a cylinder. If a belt was worn or the style of the dress indicated a division between skirt and top, it was at hip level. The most shocking aspect of the new fashion (from the older generation's perspective) was the short skirt, which finished above the knee for the first time in 1925. Geometric Art Deco patterns were popular. Hair was worn short, originally bobbed – cut close to the nape of the neck, with the tips of the ears visible, and then shingled – very short, shaped to the head and tapering to a point at the back. Finally, the extreme was reached with the ultra short Eton crop, derived from the schoolboy style – short back and sides, exposing the ears. Ladies even went to gentlemen's barbers to get their hair cut. The emphasis was on practicality and convenience. Hair pins and extravagant hats were replaced by the simple skull-covering cloche hat. It was simply not possible to wear the new style hats over old fashioned hair styles. Young ladies shocked their parents' generation still further in the twenties by smoking cigarettes and putting on make-up in public for the first time.

In the thirties, the waistline moved back to its proper place and a more feminine, slender look was in vogue. Skirts became longer. Hair was grown and the permanent wave or 'perm' became fashionable.

Men generally wore suits. The lounge suit, usually double breasted, was standard kit for the younger generation. For the smart young man, particularly from the working classes, the sharp suit, resembling styles worn in contemporary movies, was the only way to impress the ladies. The smart white shirt, often with a striped club-style tie, completed the outfit – predating the style of the Mods in the early sixties.

Although the seaside was the ideal place to show off fashion in general, there were some styles specific to the seaside. In the twenties, young gentlemen at leisure, or those who aspired to be, wore blazers, either navy with a club or college badge or striped (24). The outfit would have been accompanied by flannel trousers, either white or light grey, and completed with stylish, co-respondent (two-tone) shoes in brown and white or cream. Oxford bags enjoyed a brief spell of fashion in the late twenties. These were hugely exaggerated baggy trousers up to thirty-two inches wide! The craze began when Oxford undergraduates started wearing them over sports clothes to meet strict dress codes for

Holidays were a great time for dressing up. Unlike today, people wore their smartest clothes in their leisure time. The family album shots on the next three pages give a flavour of how people looked on holiday.

24 Above: Walter Floyd on holiday at Camber Sands in Sussex, 1930s. He is wearing the uniform of the smart young man at leisure – a blazer and flannels. (Elsie Floyd)

25 Left: Julia Braggs and Doris Bowler at Southend in 1935. (Julia Braggs)

26 These three are wearing typical outfits for the era. The two gentlemen have blazers and the lady a cloche hat.

27 Another group on the promenade. Note the short dresses worn by the ladies and the low waistline and belt worn by the lady with the scarf.

28 Stepping out thirties style – typically smart attire for a typically cold seaside day.

dining in hall when time did not allow them to change. By the early thirties, they had disappeared. The general trend throughout the inter-war period was for less formal leisurewear. On the beach, in hot weather, the jackets were often dispensed with and trousers held up by belts with open neck shirts were preferred by the young. By the thirties, this convention became acceptable off the beach as well. Young men rarely wore hats. This earned them the collective title of the 'hatless brigade' from members of the older generation, who still wore suits, with a hat, collar and tie, whatever the temperature.

For the fashionable sunbathers in the South of France, the thirties brought blue and white striped pullovers, sailor style. The Prince of Wales, who often set the trend in contemporary men's fashion, was seen sporting one by Vogue in the early thirties.

One of the most colourful ladies' fashions of the inter-war period was beach pyjamas (**30**). These were brightly patterned, loose-fitting bell-bottomed trousers with a backless and sleeveless top. They could be worn over the new bathing costumes. Designs were usually abstract with geometric patterns. Other variations were stripes, circles or spots. They were first introduced for the 1927 summer season. Originally they were taken up by the 'bright young things', but by the early thirties, though, the smart set had abandoned them in favour of playsuits, comprising shorts, skirt or more usually trousers and top.

As with most fashions though, beach pyjamas were soon worn by more ordinary people. They became a common sight on English beaches for most of the thirties. They could be made of silk, but more commonly of crêpe de chine, éponge (an early form of towelling) or jersey. The abstract patterns and bright colours continued. More often than not, the outfit was completed by a wide-brimmed, floppy sun hat and high-heeled shoes. Girls on coach parties took up the style with enthusiasm. Later in the thirties, beach pyjamas were joined by short-legged trousers, fastening at the side, made of wool or linen. Later still, cotton dungarees made an appearance.

29 Dancing at Bournemouth's pavilion. Note the ladies' backless evening gowns and the gentlemen's white tie evening dress. (Bournemouth Tourism)

30 Beach pyjamas as a fashion started in 1927. Originally they were worn by the smart set that holidayed at the Riviera. They were, however, soon taken up by ordinary people and were a common sight on British beaches for most of the thirties. This advertisement from Plummer's department store in Hastings (1933) is typical of the era. The lady in the centre on the bottom row completes the look with a floppy, wide-brimmed hat. (Hastings & St Leonards Observer)

Central Parade and Wish Tower, Eastbourne.

31 Summer fashions on parade at Eastbourne in the twenties.

Footwear on the beach for ladies was either rubber slip-ons worn in the water, plimsolls or sandals. Ladies still wore Panama hats in the early thirties but abandoned them by the end of the decade, preferring headscarves or no headwear at all.

Another fashionable beach accessory that started life in the twenties was the beach towel. Bright colours and striking abstract patterns prevailed. By the thirties, the sun ray pattern was a common design. Occasionally, these would be very large and fitted with a drawstring at the top to make a body-covering wrap that could be used for changing.

Another thirties innovation was the backless sundress, allowing ladies to absorb the sun's rays after changing out of their swimming costumes.

After the sun had gone down, the elegance of evening dress replaced the flamboyance of the blazers and beach pyjamas in England. Most of the larger hotels still insisted on dressing for dinner. Men wore double-breasted dinner jackets with wing-collared dress shirts and black bow ties. Some pavilion ballrooms expected nothing less than full white tie evening dress – Fred Astaire style, complete with top hat. Ladies wore evening dresses. In the twenties, these followed daywear fashions and were invariably short. By the thirties, they reached ankle length again and the striking backless gown was 'in' (**29**).

For those less inclined to eat in their hotels, or for those stopping at one of the many boarding houses, lounge suits were usually worn in the evening to the theatre, cinema or restaurant.

When the war came in 1939, this world was lost forever. The blazer disappeared and dress codes became less restrictive. However, even in the days of the Teddy Boys, suits were still considered essential for a night out on the town, whether at home or on holiday.

6 Sun Worship

The sun was the most ubiquitous image of the inter-war period. It appeared on almost anything from garden gates to cigarette cases. It can surely be no coincidence that the late twenties and early thirties saw sunbathing reach the level of popularity it enjoys today.

The rise of sunbathing was a complete reversal of taste from the mid-Victorian era when it was fashionable to stay out of the sun. Victorian ladies carried parasols out of fear of the effects of the sun on their delicate complexions and leisured gentlemen avoided the sun for being mistaken for farm workers or fishermen for whom a tan was obligatory as a result of their occupations. Tennyson, in the poem *Aonea*, based on Greek mythology, described the hero, Paris, as 'white breasted as a star', assuming that contemporary Victorian attitudes were held in Ancient Greece.

However, towards the end of the Victorian era, things were beginning to change. The growth in popularity of outdoor sports such as tennis, swimming and cycling, particularly with women, meant that acquiring the semblance of a tan was inevitable on those parts of the body that were exposed to the sun. It then became socially acceptable. Changes in working practices resulting in the decline of agricultural work and the growth of factory work also meant that a sun tan lost the association with manual labour that it had hitherto held.

After gaining social acceptance, it was not long before the medical profession started to exploit the beneficial effects of the sun. In 1903, Auguste Rollier opened the 'sunshine clinic' in the Alps for the treatment of tuberculosis. It was not until the 1920s, however, that the practice of deliberately exposing the body to the sun for the sole purpose of acquiring a tan became fashionable.

The craze began when the artistic community first started to inhabit the Riviera in the summers of the early 1920s. Formerly, the Riviera had been fashionable only for the winter season. Fitzgerald, Hemmingway, Léger and Picasso had all stayed at Gerald Murphy's villa at Cap d'Antibes – one of the first to have a flat roof for sunbathing. By the mid-twenties, the seasons had reversed and Riviera summers were in full swing.

By the late 1920s, the Riviera had become simply the place to be for the young, fashionable and, of course, rich. Film stars, writers, singers and artists mixed with the 'bright young things' from the smart set in London under its brilliant sun. Riviera summers were an endless experience of delightful leisure and pure enjoyment in a world from which all the realities of normal life had been banished. The long summer days gave the 'bright young things' plenty of opportunity to soak up the sun's rays and turn their skins brown. Swimming and diving were the sports enthusiastically pursued. As the long days wore on into beautiful summer evenings, the casino at Cannes, 'Le Palm Beach', became a popular retreat. Cocktails were drunk throughout the night and the next day it all started again.

Get alluring SUN-TAN quickly-safely

Don't waste precious holiday hours *hoping* to get brown. Be the envy of all your friends. Use Rayfilta — and win the race for glowing sun-tan! It's simply marvellous.

Quite new — a jelly!

Rayfilta is a non-greasy jelly containing an expensive ingredient which cuts out all the burning, blistering part of sunlight, and only lets through the healthy bronzing rays. It is invisible immediately it is applied to the skin.

Gives you 'brown-satin skin'

By using Rayfilta you can obtain a skin like brown satin in the shortest possible time. Absolutely non-greasy, beautifully clean to use. Won't spoil clothes and swim-suits or grow hair. Wonderful powder foundation. Harmless for young and old—splendid for the kiddies.

RAYFILTA
NON-GREASY
SUN TAN JELLY

Tubes 1/3 and 2/6
(Family Size))

32 Early sunbathers had used olive oil to prevent their skin turning red, but by the thirties, numerous tanning creams were available. Summer editions of thirties magazines were full of advertisements such as this one. Note the lady's costume has a cut-away panel at the side as an aid to getting an all-over tan.

By now, a suntan meant the lady or gentleman in question had the leisure and money to invest in expensive holidays at the Riviera. The social cachet of the sun-bronzed skin was firmly established. It was not long before the craze spread to England's holidaymakers and the sight of bodies grilling slowly in the British sun to varying degrees of success was common place at its seaside resorts. Sunbathing in England was taken very seriously by some in the thirties. Those that embraced the inter-war crazes of hiking and nudism saw sunbathing as another health fad and took to it with enthusiasm. Just how seriously is shown by this extract from *The Health and Nature Cure Handbook* (published 1931):

> There are several ways of exposing the naked body to the solar rays: (a) outdoors, in a standing position, moving about; (b) outdoors in a reclining position, with the head, eyes and back of the neck shaded; (c) outdoors, as in (b), but in a 'sun-box', which screens the bather on three sides from the wind, and the head in particular from the sun; (d) reclining on a bed in a ventilated glass solarium, the head, eyes and back of the neck shaded, and a cold wet cloth over the head, when indicated. The last two mentioned methods are the more scientific.[1]

In spite of these 'scientific methods' and much documented evidence of the beneficial properties of sunlight, many local authorities were slow to catch onto the idea of providing facilities for sunbathing. At the time the above article was written, any man bathing in the Serpentine wearing only shorts would have been fined. Only on Brighton beach were men not required to cover their upper body.

The early sunbathers in France had used olive oil to prevent their skins from turning red. By the end of the twenties, holidaymakers in England used one of the many tanning creams enthusiastically advertised in the summer editions of magazines (**32**).

The sun was used extensively to sell holiday destinations to potential visitors. Resorts vied with each other quoting sunshine statistics and even ultraviolet counts. Paradoxically, ultraviolet rays were thought to be health-giving. The sun ray motif found its way into advertisements for the resorts (**33, 34**). 'Sun Ray' became a popular guest house name and the Southern Railway coined the phrase 'Sunny South' in its advertisements.

The use of the sun in art dates back to the earliest times, but it acquired new meaning in the thirties. It now symbolized youth, health, wealth and leisure – ideal for a fashion motif. The most common form was the sun ray, a semicircle, more usually a quadrant, with stylized lines radiating from its centre. The sun ray adorned powder compacts, cigarette cases and jewellery (**35, 36**). Smoking and putting on make-up in public was still considered daringly modern for young ladies in the early thirties. What could be more fashionable than to take a cigarette out of a sun ray patterned case, place it in a long telescopic holder and casually pose with it strolling along the prom, or reclining in a deck chair on the sand?

The sun ray motif was popular with men's fashion too, featuring on cufflinks and tie clips and even on two-tone co-respondent shoes.

---

[1] From an article by Gordon Pitcairn-Knowles in *The Nature Cure Handbook* published by the Nature Cure Educational Association in 1931.

.....A Mediterranean
Watering Place.....

on the English Channel ... where healthy pine-laden breezes and day after day of warm sunshine give you a new health and vigour ... Take the facts of Bournemouth's amazing reputation for fair weather and a perfect climate — then go there for your holiday. You'll enjoy the unrivalled facilities for every kind of sport — the many interesting and beautiful walks into the historic " Hardy " country ... while the evenings offer a most comprehensive programme of amusement and entertainment.

Write for Winter Literature and Guide free from the Town Clerk, Room 28a, Town Hall, Bournemouth.

BOURNEMOUTH

The Centre of Health and Sunshine.

The sun was used extensively to sell English resorts to holidaymakers. This advertisement for Bournemouth – 'a Mediterranean Watering Place' – uses the sun ray motif (33, left) and that for Hastings (34, below) – 'Travel Sunwards to Hastings' suggests taking the train to a sun-drenched paradise, to escape the undoubted grime of the city. (Bournemouth Tourism [left] and Hastings Borough Council [below])

TRAVEL SUNWARDS ɼO
HASTINGS
AND ST. LEONARDS

A Postcard to Sec., Room 18, Boro' Assoc., Hastings, will bring per return a handsome booklet (free) about this delightful all-round
:: :: Resort, justly called :: ::

BRITAIN'S BEST TONIC
Great Pageant at Battle Abbey, July 14th-16th.

The sun-ray motif was incredibly popular in contemporary fashion accessories, such as the cigarette case (35, right), also featuring an Aztec temple (or space ship?) and the cufflinks (36, below). (Both pictures by Diane Harris)

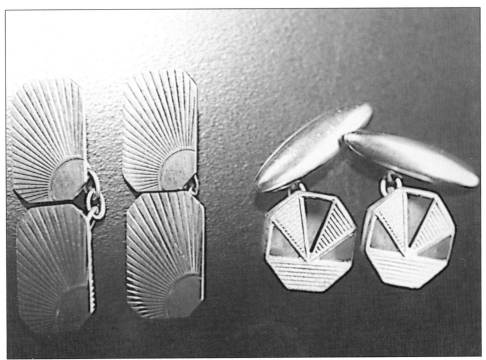

37 The Solarium at Bournemouth's Pier Approach baths opened in 1937. There you could still get a tan even when the English weather lived up to its reputation. Almost certainly, the artificial sun lamps were far from healthy. (Bournemouth Tourism)

The sun ray also found its way to suburbia on the garden gate or stained glass windows of many of the new semi-detached houses being built at astonishing rates in the era. The effect of sun worship on the architecture of the thirties was, however, much more far-reaching than mere decoration. The modern house with its flat roof began slowly to grace the English countryside from the late twenties. Although popular with the fashionable, it was never fully accepted by the public at large. However, the provision of sun decks on private homes in a country not known for its hot weather is firm evidence of the seriousness with which the cult of sun worship was taken. Osbert Lancaster poked fun with a cartoon showing a couple sunbathing on the flat roof of their 'twentieth-century functional' house, who were just about to dash indoors to avoid the inevitable summer downpour.

Designers of swimming pools, as we shall see later, also ensured that provision was made for sunbathing as well as bathing by adding sundecks and terraces to their buildings (see Chapter 8). Architects made sure people could enjoy the sun, even when the weather was cold, by using 'Vita' glass designed to let in the maximum amount of sunlight in both houses and public buildings. In 1937, the Sun Lounge was built at Hastings, situated on the promenade facing the sea and below the town's modernistic Marine Court Flats. It has vast areas of glass arranged in a semicircle giving customers plenty of opportunity to soak up the sun, even when the coastal winds are strong, while they sip their afternoon tea or eat their ice creams. Bournemouth's new Pier Approach Baths, opened in 1937, had a solarium (**37**) where sunbathers could enjoy 'the equivalent of natural sunlight' when the weather was less bright. The use of sun lamps at home for topping up the tan was also popular.

38 A newspaper advertisement from 1933, showing a selection of typical men's bathing wear. Although the upper body is still covered, these garments have large areas scooped out to maximise exposure to the sun. (Hastings & St Leonards Observer)

The craze for sunbathing brought a more lasting fashion in the ever-changing shape of sunglasses. In the twenties and thirties, they were characteristically simple in design, usually styled in plastic, then a new material, with round lenses.

Sun worship also influenced mainstream fashion in the form of the backless evening dress in the late twenties and early thirties. Young ladies could now show off their tanned skin to good effect after the sun had gone down. Their dresses were often worn with a string of pearls hanging down the back in brilliant contrast to the tanned skin.

The craze for sunbathing changed bathing costumes out of all recognition. It would simply not have been possible to get a tan wearing the cumbersome costumes of the Edwardian age. The classic male costume, a one-piece affair in cotton with legs and sleeves, often decorated with horizontal stripes was laughed out of existence. Men's costumes now had shorter shorts and straps replaced sleeves, but the torso was still covered (**38**). In the twenties, plain colours

39 How things have changed! A fashion parade at St Leonards Bathing Pool in the mid-thirties shows just how far swimwear had come since the Victorian age. Of the ladies in modern dress, three are in beach pyjamas and three in the latest one-piece swimming costumes.

40 Julia Braggs at Pevensey Bay with a friend. (Julia Braggs)

41 By the end of the thirties the bra and shorts style of bathing costume joined the one-piece. The word 'bikini' was not used until after the Second World War. (Photograph taken by A.E. Raddy; courtesy of Rex Raddy)

42 Bathing hats were just the thing to complement the new swimming costumes, particularly if you swam as well as sunbathed. Note the references to Riviera resorts, which were highly fashionable with the 'bright young things'; however, it is more likely that these bathing hats were worn on British beaches.

were generally preferred. Black, navy, maroon or royal blue were the norm. In the early thirties the top was often a different colour to the shorts and occasionally striped. The shorts became shorter still. Men in continental resorts in the twenties began to wear trunks and gradually the trunks became shorter, although still of the mini shorts style. By the thirties, trunks became acceptable on British beaches, although some resorts still refused to permit bare chests. Jantzen – the fashion leader – responded with the 'topper' – trunks onto which a detachable top could be fitted. Even swimsuits, which included a vest, were designed to expose the maximum amount of the wearer's back to the sun. By the end of the thirties, trunks had finally been accepted at most British beaches. The usual style no longer resembled a pair of shorts. A horizontal line at groin level could be seen with a belt, although the navel was still covered. Advances in technology also helped the design of more becoming beachwear when lastex, rubber combined with cotton or rayon, was introduced from America.

Ladies' swimwear followed a similar evolution, although more dramatic. As the First World War approached, the frilly body covering bathing wear of the Victorian lady had already disappeared in favour of a one-piece affair with almost knee-length shorts. More flattering bathing wear, especially when wet, had become increasingly important as many resorts dispensed with bathing machines and segregated bathing. By the early twenties, these outmoded practices had all but disappeared. Bathing costumes were now either one piece with shorts and a sleeveless top combined or two-piece with a tunic partially covering mid-thigh-length knickers. The costumes, like the men's, were generally made of cotton at the beginning of the decade but this was soon to be replaced by the more flattering machine-knitted wool. Machine-knitted wool may not sound very comfortable for swimming, but it was far more figure-hugging than cotton. Style followed contemporary fashion with the waistline being around the hips. Costumes could be plain or patterned with stripes being the most popular, although bold Art Deco styles were not unknown. The outfits were usually finished off with a headscarf. Bathing hats made of rubber (**42**) became popular in the late twenties, replacing the headscarves. These were ideally suited to wearing over the current short hairstyles, the bob, the shingle and the extreme Eton crop. These hats usually were covered with a moulded design, sometimes abstract, sometimes floral, and fastened under the chin by a rubber strap. Towards the end of the twenties the two-piece costume had almost died out, being replaced by a one-piece with an overskirt. Although attractive out of water, these ladies would have looked less so when wet, as the materials used for the costumes would have still appeared bedraggled.

All this changed in 1929, when Jantzen launched 'the suit that changed bathing into swimming'. This was a simple one-piece affair, made of a figure hugging material with shorts finishing just below the top of the leg and no overskirt. In the years that followed, costumes became more revealing, allowing for maximum exposure to the sun. Very soon backless costumes with large areas scooped out of the sides were worn with narrow shoulder straps or halter necks – a high panel on the front of the costume being tied around the neck leaving the back and shoulders completely exposed. By the mid-thirties, the one-piece costume had been joined by the bra and shorts style (**41**). Towards the end of the thirties, beachwear had become sufficiently fashionable to demand its own Paris show, the 'Fête de l'Eau'. *Picture Post* in 1939 described the scene:

43 Elsie Floyd (née Mercer) at Hope Cove, Devon, wearing a typical thirties bathing costume. (Elsie Floyd)

There was a time when a bathing costume was something made of hard-wearing cotton, dyed navy blue with a high neck line and button shoulder straps; something which you wore shamefacedly in your hurried trip from bathing hut to sea. Nowadays, it is as much a creation as a model gown. It is something in which you show yourself as much as possible – and in which as much of yourself as is permissible is shown. Paris, at any rate, considers the bathing costume a sufficiently important branch of women's dress for a Fête de l'Eau to be held each year, at which only swimming creations are shown.[2]

As well as two-piece bathing costumes, cork soled shoes became popular fashion accessories towards the end of the decade. The word 'bikini' was never used before the war. It was taken from the name of an island in the Pacific on which the Americans tested an atomic bomb.

Sun worship was one twenties fad that outlived the decade. In fact it was made all the more accessible for the majority of the public when cheap air travel opened the gateway to Spain and the opportunity of guaranteed sun. It acquired a new fashion status in the sixties and seventies, but it is finally being challenged today as we have come to realize that the sun's rays may not be as healthy and beneficial as was first imagined. The sun ray motif, however, did not survive the war. Its similarity to the Japanese 'rising sun' saw to that.

[2] From 'On the Beach in Paris', in *Picture Post*, 15 July 1939. Reproduced courtesy of IPC Magazines Ltd.

7 Concrete and Chromium Plate

The unprecedented increase in the number of people who were able to take a holiday away from home by the sea had far reaching consequences on the appearance of the English coast. Firstly, the resorts had to be adapted and improved to cope with the increased numbers. Secondly, the inter-war years were the time in which local councillors began to assume the responsibility of running the seaside towns as commercial enterprises. In Victorian and Edwardian times, it had been private enterprise that took the lead. In the inter-war years, the local councillors became directors of their towns. Ever increasing sums of ratepayers' money seemed to be available to spend. Blackpool, not surprisingly, spent the most: £1½ million on a seven-mile promenade, £300,000 on indoor baths; £75,000 on an open air pool; and £250,000 on the entirely new Stanley Park. Brighton extended her promenade six miles to the new resort of Saltdean, added a new outdoor pool and revamped the aquarium. Bournemouth spent £250,000 on a new pavilion in 1929 and opened the new Pier Approach Baths in 1937. Hastings spent £100,000 on the White Rock Pavilion, £180,000 on a new promenade and an underground car park and well over £150,000 on new swimming facilities. These figures might not seem huge by today's standards, but in those days, you could have bought a brand new semi-detached house for as little as £500. There was open competition between the resorts over the amounts spent. Guidebooks trumpeted: 'visit the new £100,000 baths'. Statistics such as the length of the new seafront were proudly boasted of. New promenades and coastal defences in concrete were considered the most important part of any modernization programme.

Seaside towns have always been in a world of their own, a chance to escape the realities of daily life for one or two weeks of the year. They are, or at least attempt to be, a veritable pleasure palace by the sea, offering their visitors dazzling temptations and entertainment. As such, their architecture has often leaned towards the fanciful and exaggerated. This has been the tradition ever since the Brighton Pavilion was built for the Prince Regent in 1820 (**44**). Nash's design was oriental in flavour, with its famous 'onion' domes. The interior was in Chinese style. The Pavilion was quite unlike any building of its era. Its influence on seaside architecture from that date onwards was profound. The style of the Pavilion found its way onto the Victorian and Edwardian pier in the Baroque flourishes in wrought iron and in the oriental onion domes of the kiosks, bandstands and pavilions.

With so much money to spend and local councils so willing to spend it, many resorts were literally transformed in the twenties and thirties. At the beginning of the twenties, seaside architecture followed the traditions of the Victorian age. A proposal for improvements to ageing baths at Hastings even as late as 1926 still copied the exotic style

44 The Brighton Pavilion, a veritable Oriental pleasure palace. It was built by Nash for the Prince Regent in 1820 and was an inspiration to pier builders and seaside architects for over one hundred years. (Diane Harris)

of the Brighton Pavilion. The new pier pavilion and bandstand at Worthing, built in 1925/26, used the traditional seaside style. In most new building work in the twenties there was a simpler feel although, for the most part, the design was along traditional lines. The popular architectural style of the day was the classical or Neo-Georgian and this was well represented at the seaside. The Winter Gardens at Weston-super-Mare, which opened in 1927, followed this style, making extensive use of pillars (**colour plate 17**). The Pavilion at Bournemouth, opened in 1929 (**45**), used the Georgian style, mainly in red brick, but with rather grand square-looking pillars in Portland stone and concrete surrounding most of the building. Other styles were used. Hastings' White Rock Pavilion (1928) is in a Spanish style (**46**). None of these buildings were in any way 'modern'.

By the thirties there was a dramatic shift in tastes. The purpose was still the same, to create a fantasy world where the ordinary and dull would be banished, but the shape of that world was to change beyond recognition. No longer was the oriental pleasure palace the inspiration, but the sophistication of the South of France and the ocean liner. The idea was to bring the style of the buildings of continental Europe to our shores, so that the middle and working classes could lap up the atmosphere without the expense and the perceived dubious morals associated with the 'bright young things' of the smart set. To see how much things had changed over the inter-war period, take a look at the Casino at Blackpool. The original Casino at Blackpool's Pleasure Beach (**47**) was built in 1913 and was replaced only twenty-six years later with a new design by architect Joseph Emberton (**48**). The original was built essentially

45 *The Pavilion in Bournemouth (seen here c. 1929) uses a rather heavy Georgian style, but note the modern style sign and typical inter-war light fittings outside.*

46 *Seaside buildings, twenties style. The White Rock Pavilion, Hastings, was built in 1927 in a Spanish hacienda style. The bath chair in the foreground is perhaps indicative of the kind of resort Hastings was before Sidney Little transformed it.*

just before our period began, as there was very little seaside building during the First World War; its replacement is right at the end of our period. 'Casino' is something of a misnomer, as gambling was not permitted and both buildings were really restaurants and cafés. The original building used all the styling tricks of the Victorian and Edwardian seaside architect. It has been compared, by different authors, to an Indian palace and to a wedding cake. It is a flamboyant, distinctly over-the-top architectural indulgence in fantasy, a building designed for fun, rather than serious purpose.

The new Casino, which still stands today, is quite the opposite in style. It has virtually no applied decoration. A simple, circular form is used for the main building with a wide expanse of glass. The building is topped with a circular tower. White was the predominant colour. It is the last word in 1930s chic. In spite of its much more functional appearance, the new Casino is just as much fun as its more fancy predecessor was. This sense of fun is expressed in the tower with its concrete 'corkscrew', echoing the corkscrew staircase inside the building and providing the entrance to the Pleasure Beach. Modern architecture and construction techniques have been used to create a building that is new and exciting.

The architecture of what became known as the 'Modern Movement' was based on the principle that 'form follows function': that the outward appearance of the building should be determined solely by the intended use of its interior. This doctrine was publicized in Europe by, amongst others, the architect Le Corbusier and Head of the Bauhaus School of Art and Design, Walter Gropius. Both had designed modern buildings, even before the First World War. The majority of true modern buildings in the twenties and thirties had similar outward characteristics: flat roofs; the use of white concrete; strong geometrical shapes, particularly the cube; the use of cantilevered balconies; large expanses of glass; and, above all, an almost complete absence of any ornamentation.

Probably the finest example of a modern seaside building is the De La Warr Pavilion at Bexhill-on-Sea (**colour plate 15**). The idea for the Pavilion came from the Mayor of Bexhill, the Ninth Earl De La Warr, a socialist peer. He convinced the town councillors that the entertainment facilities of Bexhill needed to be improved to prevent it from losing the business to other resorts, and in 1933 a competition was announced to design a new pavilion in a simple and modern style. The winning entry was a design by the architects Eric Mendelsohn and Serge Chermayeff working in partnership. Mendelsohn was a German by birth, but had left his native land when Hitler came to power in 1933. Chermayeff, who emigrated from Russia, had produced some striking modern radio cabinet designs for Ekco.

The Pavilion, which was opened on 12 December 1935, fully utilized the latest techniques and building materials. A welded, steel-framed structure, a German idea used for the first time in the UK, was employed supporting plate glass walls. The effect is stunning and the Pavilion is unlike any other seaside building, even today. The building is dominated by a wonderful round staircase, which has a beautifully light feeling to it when viewed from the outside. Inside, the staircase has a magnificent modernist light fitting running almost from top to bottom (**colour plate 16**). Its balconies have a superb view of the beach and out to sea, whilst inside the building is light and airy.

The facilities of the Pavilion were extensive, including a restaurant, auditorium, library and reading room. Most typically for the thirties, a flat roof was provided for sunbathing along with a sun balcony for soaking up the sun's rays when the weather was less clement.

The Casino, Blackpool, built in 1913 (47, above) and its replacement designed by Emberton and built in 1939 (48, below). In twenty-six years, the change in tastes is remarkable. Note also the modern buildings in the restyled Pleasure Beach behind.

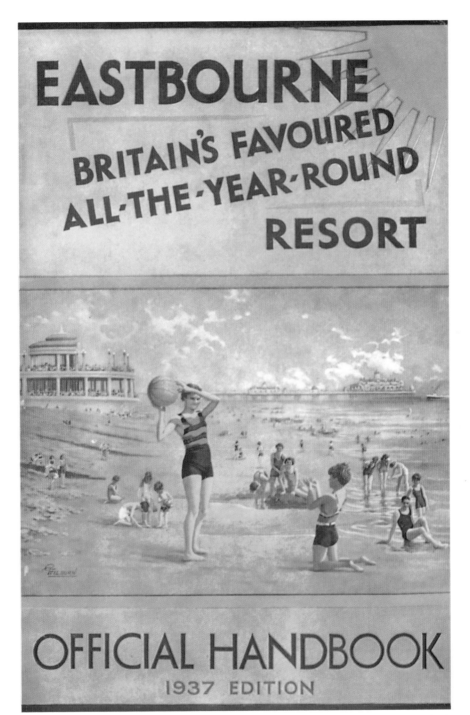

EASTBOURNE
BRITAIN'S FAVOURED ALL-THE-YEAR-ROUND RESORT

OFFICIAL HANDBOOK
1937 EDITION

1 Guidebooks were the window through which the seaside towns displayed their wares. By the thirties they were very colourful and helped to establish an image for the resorts. The next three pages show a selection of 1930s examples. Here, an Eastbourne guidebook from 1937. (Borough of Eastbourne Tourism, Leisure and Amenities)

WESTON
SUPER – MARE

2 Weston-super-Mare guidebook, 1939. (North Somerset Council)

3 Isle of Man guidebook, 1933. (Isle of Man Department of Tourism and Leisure)

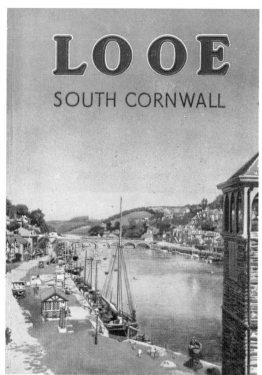

4 Looe guidebook, 1939. (Caradon District Council)

5 The Blackpool Illuminations ran for most years during the inter-war period. People were fascinated by the possibilities of electric power. The illuminations provided a colourful way of extending the holiday season into the autumn.

6 An illuminated car, Blackpool. Most resorts were losing their trams in the inter-war era. Blackpool was the only resort to make its trams a special attraction.

7 The next four pictures show the fascination of Cornwall. Here, the power and majesty of the sea at Penzance.

8 The primitive fishing fleet at Falmouth. Actually this picture is Edwardian, but things would have been little different in the twenties.

9 Sennen Cove. This postcard seems to sum up the appeal of Cornwall: its remoteness, picturesque views, genuine old atmosphere and beaches ideal for secluded sunbathing.

10 Surf riding at Newquay in 1933. (Newquay Tourism and Marketing Office)

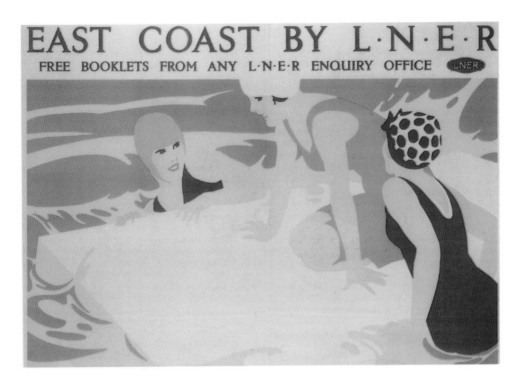

11 The LNER was particularly adept at capturing the holiday spirit in their poster campaigns. Their 'East Coast by LNER' posters helped promote a youthful and attractive image for the whole of the east coast. (National Railway Museum/Science and Society Picture Library)

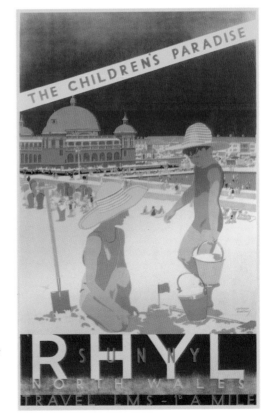

12 The LMS ran a similar poster campaign for the opposite side of the country. This image of Rhyl in North Wales is particularly endearing. (National Railway Museum/ Science and Society Picture Library)

13 Streamlined style and stained glass! Some caravans also had leaded lights. (Steven Braggs)

L·N·E·R CAMPING COACHES in England and Scotland

Accommodation for six persons from £2·10·0 per week
Ask for details at any L·N·E·R Station or Office

14 LNER's answer to the caravan: the camping coach. (National Railway Museum/Science and Society Picture Library)

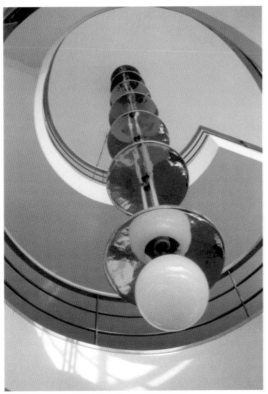

The ultimate in seaside sophistication: Mendelssohn and Chermayeff's De La Warr Pavilion at Bexhill-on-Sea (15, above), and modernist light fitting (16, left). This is arguably the finest modern seaside building ever built. (Diane Harris)

17 The Winter Garden, Weston-super-Mare, built in 1927 in classical style.

18 Modernism was by no means the only building style used at the seaside in the thirties. Some resorts stuck to the traditional seaside style following the legacy of the Brighton Pavilion. This is the Bandstand at Eastbourne, built in 1935. (Diane Harris)

Ford V·8

To or from the swimming-pool there's only one way to travel " de luxe," in the luxury-car for the economically-inclined, the FORD V-8, that does so much, so easily, so well, and so inexpensively! The Local Ford Dealer invites you to know all about it, perhaps for the first time realising how very little this beautiful car costs, to buy, insure, run, and maintain always at its best. Literature on Request: All Prices at Works: Dealers Everywhere.

Ford V-8 Cabriolet illustrated, **£240** (£22 . 10s. Tax)

Alternative Body-Styles from £230.

ORD MOTOR COMPANY LIMITED. DAGENHAM. ESSEX. LONDON SHOWROOMS: 88 REGENT ST., W

19 Arrive at the lido in style in a new Ford V8! The advertisement dates from 1935. Outdoor swimming was unquestionably chic in the thirties. It was used extensively to market everything from motor cars to cornflakes. (Ford Motor Company)

20/21 The Jubilee Pool, Penzance, built in 1935. It was built right on the shoreline in Penzance and had to be able to withstand the full ferocity of the Cornish seas. (Left: Diane Harris; below: Steven Braggs)

22 Birnbeck, or Old Pier, Weston-super-Mare. Note the pleasure steamer leaving the pier head. Trips from Birnbeck went to Cardiff, Newport, Barry, Bristol, Clevedon, Ilfracombe and Clovelly.

23 The Connaught Theatre, Worthing – the cinematic style transferred to another building type. This building was actually converted from a cinema, bucking the trend of the time. However, its modern façade was built in 1935, when the conversion took place. (Diane Harris)

24 *The Midland Hotel, Morecambe. Note the medallion bearing the inscription: 'And hear Old Triton blow his wreathed horn', as seen from the foot of the spiral staircase. It was carved by Eric Gill and painted by Dennis Tegetmeier. (Diane Harris).*

"I'm thinking of swimming the Channel -- but not this week!"

Donald McGill's postcards had a very different take on seaside life from the ideal world of the guidebooks and railway posters. He covered all aspects of the English seaside holiday, from swimming (25, below opposite) to bathing wear (28, overleaf, top left) and fashion (29, overleaf, top right), not to mention sex (26, right) and true love (27, below). As well as the obvious humour, the cards provide an insight into the fashions of the day. The two young men on the right are smartly dressed and the young lady is wearing a typical short twenties skirt. The caption, though, would hardly be acceptable today!

"It's better to be deaf than blind!"

"I was coming all the way by Charabanc - but I 'got off' before I reached here!"

AT CLEETHORPES.
My new bathing dress
Is quite a success -
What you can't see of me
Of course you must guess!

"Just because I'm smart, the men think I'm fast!"

I've spent some jolly evenings round the bandstand

30 *The seaside holiday was a time for indulgence, as this postcard shows!*

Modernism also found a home at Brighton. In the mid-thirties, the train service between London and Brighton was vastly improved. New electric trains ran to Brighton from London six times each hour. These new trains were not only fast, but also clean and comfortable. This made commuting from a home in Brighton to work in the Metropolis an attractive proposition, particularly as rents at Brighton were considerably cheaper than London and of course the Brighton air was much healthier. To house the most fashionable of these new commuters, Wells Coates designed Embassy Court (**49**). Strangely enough, Wells Coates' earlier work also included radio cabinet design for Ekco. Wells Coates was a devotee of Le Corbusier and resolutely took the doctrine of 'form follows function' to heart. The flats were built using true functionalist principles. The interior of the flats was planned first, using the idea of maximum convenience and minimum clutter, and then the exterior was planned around it. The structure is monolithic concrete featuring wrap-round curved balconies and 'suntrap' windows. You can imagine the pleasure of relaxing on a warm Summer evening, after a hard day at the office, sitting out on the balcony, sipping a cocktail and looking out to sea. Embassy Court followed on from a similar block in Lawn Road in Hampstead, which numbered among its tenants leading modern architects and designers and the popular crime fiction writer, Agatha Christie.

Some towns were altered completely in character in the thirties. The medium-sized resort of Hastings and St Leonards is perhaps the best example. In the early part of the twenties Hastings and particularly St Leonards were very conservative. In September 1926, 3,000 of the town's residents petitioned the town council to introduce a speed limit of 10mph along the sea front – no faster than horse drawn traffic in the age of the motor car! A few months later, the town was to be changed forever. One man brought about the change: Sidney Little, the new Borough Engineer.

Little took a walk around the town before his interview for the post. He was dismayed by what he found. Hastings and St Leonards was a sleepy and slightly run-down Victorian seaside town that had yet to embrace the twentieth century. He told the interview panel that, if appointed, he would bring the town up to date. Once appointed he set out with a resolve and determination to do just that.

In the early thirties the town's tramways were ripped up to make way for a completely new promenade built in reinforced concrete. The new front was a 'double decker' with both upper and lower walkways. The lower walkway was built in a very functionalist style, but was relieved by decoration made from different coloured broken glass set into the concrete. The glass came from a large quantity of broken bottles that Little discovered on a rubbish tip. It is known as 'Bottle Alley'. The effect is striking and it looks remarkably modern given that is was built in the thirties. One could be forgiven for thinking that it was built in the sixties. An underground car park (**50**) was constructed as part of the new development. At the time it removed the eyesore of cars parked along the front – it is still there today, but is, of course, nowhere near adequate for its original task. There are also some rather futuristic concrete shelters dotted along the front (**51, 52**). He was also responsible for the design of Hastings' new bathing pool built in 1933 (see Chapter 8). It was for these developments (amongst others at Hastings) that Little earned the title of 'Concrete King'. He was later to put his skills to use in the service of the nation when he was involved in the construction of the Mulberry floating harbour used in the D-Day landings in 1944.

49 Wells Coates' Embassy Court in Brighton, photographed in 1995. It is a superb example of functionalist architecture. The interior of the building was planned first and the exterior followed on from this. (Diane Harris)

As well as Little's work, a new block of flats called Marine Court (**54**) was built at St Leonards in 1937 replacing a terrace of Victorian houses. It was described as 'a liner on land'. The inspiration for the design came from the *Queen Mary* ocean liner. Immediately below Marine Court, also in 1937, a sun lounge was built on the lower deck of the promenade. The Sun Lounge could seat up to 1,000 people. At the time, it was a major social rendezvous (see also Chapter 6).

In spite of its popularity, modernism was not to everyone's taste. Along with the new white concrete and chrome of the modern movement and its imitators, designs of a more traditional style were still finding a home by the sea. A new bandstand at Eastbourne, for example, was built in 1935 in a restrained oriental style (**colour plate 18**). It does not have the extravagance of the Brighton Pavilion, but nevertheless is still in its spirit. The building is circular. Its surface is faced entirely with bright ceramic tiles. The roof is like an onion dome that has been squashed down. It is finished in blue and topped with a large pointed spike in the form of a cone. The remainder of the structure is cream. Four pillars in the classical style support the roof.

An interesting memorial can be seen on the wall of the promenade facing the bandstand. It is to John Wesley Woodward, who was one of the musicians who played to the end when the *Titanic* went down in 1912. He is remembered here because he played with the Grand Hotel Orchestra at Eastbourne, as well as the Eastbourne Municipal Orchestra and the Duke of Devonshire's Orchestra.

Another seaside architectural development of the era and one that caused considerable alarm among commentators at the time and since, was the rapidly expanding number of

50 The underground car park at Hastings was designed by Sidney Little and opened in the 1930s. It was built to rid the seafront of the clutter of parked cars. (Steven Braggs)

Transformation of the sea front: two rather oddly futuristic shelters at Hastings, from the mid-thirties, designed by Sidney Little (51, right and 52, overleaf top), and the new Promenade at Brighton (53, overleaf bottom), which now went as far as Saltdean. This stretch is at Ovingdean. (51 & 52: Steven Braggs; 53: © image courtesy of Judges Postcards Ltd, Hastings (01424) 420919)

54 Marine Court at Hastings, built in 1937. It was described as a 'liner on land'. (Steven Braggs)

55 A fairly typical seaside bungalow of the era at Barton-on-Sea, c. 1939. (Francis Harris)

56 Stylish second homes: an 'oyster' bungalow with sun-trap windows at Pevensey Bay in Sussex. (Steven Braggs)

seaside bungalows. These were often prefabricated, containing only two or three rooms (**55**). They were sold as second homes for couples and families to use as a permanent base for their holidays. Builders often stressed the investment potential and likely rental income as major selling points. A great deal of these bungalows were poorly designed and built with little regard to their surroundings. However, there are some exceptionally fine examples. One site of particular interest is to be found at Pevensey Bay in Sussex. A development was built there in the later thirties based on Swedish designs. There are two principal types, although the catalogue produced at the time listed numerous varieties. The most basic design – known locally as 'oyster bungalows' – have a large curved section at the front, forming the main room with windows all round and a double front door in the style of a French window (**56**). The cooking and sleeping quarters are situated behind this in a box-like structure. The bungalows are also known as 'sun traps' because of the amount of sunlight let in by their large front windows. The second type is a more boxy structure with a flat roof and typical thirties-style windows, with horizontal glazing bars. The original development was to have had shops and a cinema. Sadly, the war intervened and the cinema was never built, although development was continued after peace returned.

Seaside architecture is, however, not at its best in blocks of flats and car parks, but in the buildings of the pleasure industry: the lido and the pier, the cinema and the holiday camp. These subjects, however, deserve chapters to themselves.

8 The Lido

No other building is so evocative of inter-war holidays than the lido or open air swimming pool. The lido crystallizes the spirit of the thirties: healthy, youthful outdoor exercise; the clean lines of modern architecture; the worship of the sun; and the cult of leisure, newly discovered by the first real mass consumers. As with most twentieth century fads, the open-air pool did not originate in the period of its greatest popularity; the word 'lido', though, probably did. It comes from the Italian resort, the Venice Lido, which was highly fashionable with the 'bright young things' from the early twenties onwards. It was an attempt to bring continental chic to more mundane settings, not only at UK seaside resorts, but also to the major urban sprawls as well. In 1939, London had no less than sixty-seven pools within a ten-mile radius of Charing Cross.

Several factors came together in the inter-war years to spark off an almost insatiable appetite for outdoor swimming pools. Swimming itself was a highly fashionable sport throughout the period. It had been popular as early as 1875, when Captain Webb swam across the Channel, but was to take on a new significance from the twenties onwards. 1926 saw the first woman, Miss Gertrude Ederle, swim across the Channel, beating the then male record by two hours, followed by six other women in 1928. Magazines of the time were full of references to improving health and general fitness through swimming. S.G. Hedges writing in *Modern Woman* informs us that:

> The value of swimming to beauty and health can scarcely be overstated. In the first place the skin, which is so vitally concerned with health, is actually cleansed during the exercise itself. And instead of the hard, ill-proportioned muscular development which results from so many sports, swimming brings symmetrical growth and supple charm, as it builds pliant and well balanced muscles. It imposes little or no strain on the heart; it affords splendid spinal and pelvic exercise; it necessitates unusually deep breathing; and it is remarkably restful for the nerves.[1]

In another article the same author claimed that outdoor swimming in winter would see off colds and influenza and improve the complexion. There is no doubt that the population was considerably more hardy than today.

The Ford Motor Company illustrated their advertisement for the V8 (**colour plate 19**) in

---

[1] From the article 'Swimming' by S.G. Hedges in *Modern Woman,* July 1929.

57 Blackpool's classical pool, built in 1923. The classical style was favoured in lido design from the twenties onwards, following the contemporary trend in architecture.

1935 by showing the car in front of a backdrop of young people in colourful costumes on the diving board of a lido. Swimming was used to sell anything from cornflakes to Brylcreem!

As we have seen, bathing wear evolved during the twenties to give women more freedom to enjoy the new sport, and Jantzen launched their new costumes in 1929 with the slogan 'the suit that changed bathing into swimming'. Added to this, of course, was the cult of sunbathing which swept our shores in the early thirties and the general fashion for healthy outdoor pursuits which included hiking and rambling.

The popularity of swimming encouraged many local councils of seaside resorts to invest heavily in new pools as part of the general improvement of their resorts needed to cater for the dramatic increase in the numbers of holidaymakers. The intense competition between resorts gave rise to some ambitious projects. Blackpool, as with most things, was one of the first resorts to jump onto the bandwagon, spending £75,000 on a new pool, which opened in 1923 (**57**). This pool was constructed on a huge scale, no less than 376ft by 172ft (116m by 53m). It was wider at its extremities than a modern Olympic pool is long! Its architecture was described as 'Renaissance' in the *Blackpool Gazette and Herald*. The style was strongly influenced by the Classical, which was the prevailing fashion in domestic architecture at the time. There were many pillars in the Greek or Roman idiom. Indeed the author of the same piece compares the pool to the Colosseum. As well as being designed with the holidaymaker in mind, the pool was also suitable for competitions, as it had a 'championship area' of 330ft by 75ft and a diving area 15ft deep. The pool was able to accommodate 8,000 spectators as well as 1,500 bathers and had changing facilities for 600. Refreshment bars open to bathers were a feature of the pool that became virtually standard with all inter-war lidos. Bathers in the twenties had to pay 6d to enter the baths; children paid 4d. A costume could be hired for 3d and a cap or a towel for 1d. As this was still only 1923, no sundecks were provided. This would have been intolerable on a pool built ten years later. Sunbathing facilities were subsequently added in the early thirties.

At the start of the thirties, it became as essential to have a lido as it had been to have a pier forty years before for any seaside town that wanted to attract summer visitors in large numbers. By the end of the thirties, lidos were to be found at Prestatyn (opened 1922), Blackpool (1923), Plymouth (1928), Exmouth (1929), Skegness (1932), Hastings and St Leonards (1933), New Brighton and Wallasey (1934), Brighton (1935), Penzance (1935), Morecambe (1936), Weston-super-Mare (1938), to name a selection. Bournemouth actually had an indoor pool with one wall opening to give the advantages of an outdoor pool in hot weather.

As the twenties changed to the thirties, swimming pool design changed from the Classical to the modern. Some of the largest of the new pools were built at the medium sized resorts. As early as 1927, a campaign started in Hastings and St Leonards for a new outdoor pool (**58**), spearheaded by the *Hastings Observer*. A scheme was finally approved in 1931 and Sidney Little, the Borough Engineer, was commissioned to do the building. He was well versed in modern building techniques and chose to build the pool in reinforced concrete. The pool was built on a massive scale: 330ft by 90ft, nearly as big as Blackpool's. From the air, the design resembled a Greek or Roman amphitheatre, with curved, stepped terracing for spectators on one side and a curved deck for sunbathing on the other. Overall though, the style was

58 Pool life in full swing at Hastings and St Leonards. Note the diving board is made of concrete blocks. There is still some classical inspiration in the style of the pool, but on the whole it is modern and functional.

functional rather than classical. There were no Doric pillars or classical references. It represented a transitional phase in lido design. At the centre of the pool was an impressive array of diving boards up to 30ft high, constructed from blocks of concrete. The pool was opened to the public in June 1933. The Hastings and St Leonards *Official Handbook* for that year describes its many other attractions:

> One of the novelties is a café which provides an enclosure accessible only from the bathers' deck. There are three promenades viz a spacious top walk around the pool, a second screened with Vita glass to 'bottle' the sunshine in windy or cold weather, and a third, roofed, but open to the sea. Sunbathers have two special decks all to themselves. The terraces accommodate 2,000 sitting spectators, whilst the promenades afford room on gala days for double this number. Perhaps the most interesting innovation is the vari-coloured illuminations of the water *from below*... The whole structure is of reinforced concrete, faced with squares of tinted cement, most pleasing to the eye...[2]

In spite of the pool's many contemporary features, commercially it was not a success. Hastings was desperate to attract visitors. The pool was really much too big for the town. The Black Rock Pool at Brighton, built around the same time, was only half the size. Hastings' pool only made a profit in its first year of opening. As early as 1946, the town council tried to find someone to take over a lease on the pool. Eventually it was turned into a holiday camp and was finally demolished only a few years ago.

Morecambe was in a similar position to Hastings in the holiday market. Morecambe's council also decided it needed a large outdoor pool to compete with nearby Blackpool. A new pool (**59**) was built in 1936 on the site of the former ship breaking business of T.W. Ward Ltd. The ship breakers had long been considered an eyesore to the town, but paradoxically were something of an attraction. Many visitors paid to go on board the doomed ocean liners and warships. This time Morecambe's councillors made sure that they outdid Blackpool. The pool was truly massive, 396ft by 110ft. It was called the Super Swimming Stadium. The pool was designed by architects Cross and Sutton and built by Sir Lindsey Parkinson. The style was uncompromisingly modern. Ostensibly, it was built from reinforced concrete, like the pool at Hastings. However, 500,000 old fashioned bricks were used in the construction. The statistics of the materials used make awesome reading. As well as the bricks, there were 15,000 cubic yards of concrete, 450 tons of steel reinforcement, 2,000 square yards of granolithic flooring, $5\frac{1}{2}$ miles of pipes, 12 miles of electrical wiring and 400 lights.

Morecambe's new pool had problems right from the start. The Council was sued, unsuccessfully as it turned out, when a boy slipped on the new pool's non-slip steps and broke his front teeth. More seriously, a leak had appeared in the sea wall that formed the basin, in which the pool was set, even before construction of the pool itself began. The cause of the leak was never established and repair work never really cured the problem. This meant

---

[2] *Hastings & St Leonards Official Handbook* for 1933, reproduced by permission of Hastings Borough Council.

59 There are no doubts that Morecambe's new pool, built in 1936, is modern. In spite of the white concrete look, it was actually built partly in brick and then cement-rendered.

that sea-water could leak into the pool at high tide and the water from the pool could escape at low tide. In spite of its problems the pool did go on to play host to the Miss Great Britain contests after the war, but was eventually demolished in the seventies.

One of the most unusual and pleasing designs of the era was the Jubilee Pool at Penzance, designed by Captain F. Latham, the Borough Engineer (**colour plates 20 and 21**). The pool was opened in 1935, the year of King George V's Silver Jubilee. It was built right on the shore line at Penzance and had to be designed to cope with the full ferocity of the Cornish seas. The pool is of irregular shape because of its unique location. In spite of the design of the pool, straight edges have been avoided and gentle curves make it a most pleasant environment. A contemporary guide book tells us that:

> In many respects the design is unique architecturally, partly from a point of view of necessity in conforming with existing conditions of wave elements and rocks which controlled the outline. Streamlines have been used to the greatest advantage in meeting the direction of the storm waves, while a Cubist style has been adopted in the interior in providing diving platforms and steps.... The whole pool is surrounded by high streamlined sea walls terraced up within the interior so as to give aspect and effect. They also serve to strengthen the structure.[3]

[3] From an official guide to Penzance from the 1930s, reproduced by permission of Penwith District Council.

60 The unique semicircular diving platform at Weston-super-Mare. In spite of being listed, it was demolished in the 1980s. (Photograph by Pete Warrilow, reproduced courtesy of his grandson, Pete Warrilow)

The 'high streamlined sea walls' also protect swimmers from strong, offshore winds and form terraces for spectators. Unlike most of the seaside lidos built in this period, the pool still stands today and is in excellent condition.

By the mid thirties a standard formula for lido design had emerged. Most pools were rectangular, although oval shapes were also common. Decks for sunbathing and separate cafés for bathers and spectators were also provided. The most important of the lido's buildings was the engine room that kept the pool supplied with clean water. Much was made of the purity of water in new pools by guidebooks and contemporary advertising, suggesting that this was not always the case. Most pools of the era had a cascade or fountain. On hot days bathers could climb on to it and watch other swimmers. The fountain also served to aerate the water. Slides were also featured; a double slide or water chute was provided at the Skegness Pool. The diving boards, though, were perhaps the most stylish of the features. Some pools had very elaborate diving platforms. The one at Western-super-Mare had a semicircular platform to which boards at varying heights were mounted (**60**). This pool also had the unusual feature of a gently sloping beach area. However, it was in other respects conservative for a pool built in 1938, for the classical style was used in preference to the modern.

One particularly pleasing example of the modern style is the Saltdean Lido (**61**), which happily still stands today. Saltdean is a suburb of Brighton which was developed extensively in the thirties and promoted to potential investors as 'The Coming Resort'. Saltdean itself has many fine buildings, built in the Hollywood Modern style – white walls and green roofs – popular in many seaside developments of the era. Saltdean's lido was designed by the architect, R.W.H. Jones, who also designed the stylish Ocean Hotel in the same suburb.

The pool itself is situated near the coastline. It is relatively small, offering provision for only 500 bathers. The main building behind is a two-storey block, featuring a café with curved metal windows in its centre. Forming curved wings on either side of the café are the changing rooms on the ground floor and the sun terraces above these. The café resembles the bridge of an ocean liner. The effect is heightened by the presence of white curved metal railings on top of the café and in front of the terraces. Inspiration for the design appears to have been contemporary liner and aircraft design. No doubt, the nearby De La Warr Pavilion at Bexhill-on-Sea also had its influence. The pool itself has the popular features of a cascade in the centre and a diving board with curved railings styled to match the design of the main building. The design was well received by the contemporary architectural press.

One thing that may appear strange to the modern reader is not the popularity of the lido itself, but why they were so popular *at seaside towns*? Certainly, people had come to expect the same public facilities on holiday as they enjoyed at home. Surely, though, if they wanted to go swimming, what was wrong with the sea? What may seem even stranger is that most seaside lidos were built only a few hundred yards away from, if not actually on, the beach itself and they were filled with salt water from the sea. The answer lies in the prevailing attitude towards bathing. This was still the era of bathing restrictions and added charges. The bathing machine had ceased to be used by most people before the First World War, but the attitudes that first brought it into use died hard. It was still common for councils to insist bathers made use of and paid for the regulation council bathing huts or cubicles and some

61 *The Saltdean Lido, photographed in 1995. Built in 1938, it possibly represents the apogee of lido style. The influence of contemporary aircraft style is clear in the shape of the café. (Steven Braggs)*

62 Happy bathers at Cliftonville Pool near Margate. Note the ladies' bathing hats.

still charged bathers for the privilege of erecting their own bathing tents on the beach. At Bournemouth, the charges were 6d per half-hour to hire a bathing tent or 9d daily to use your own. At Eastbourne, you were required to pay 6d to use a corporation tent. 'Free bathing', as it was known, was only available from certain places or at certain times of the day. At Bournemouth, for example, you could only bathe without charge before 8 a.m. The practice of so called 'mackintosh bathing' was usually frowned upon and technically could result in a fine. In the thirties this involved changing into bathing wear in the hotel and walking to the beach, often only across the road, wearing a mackintosh which was then discarded on the beach. At Eastbourne in 1937 'mackintosh bathing' was permitted, but a charge of 3d was levied, which included the use of a cloakroom. Actually changing under the mackintosh or in the car parked just opposite the beach was considered even worse.

Bathers had to overcome still worse restrictions. It was quite common for council officials to decide that the weather was too 'rough' for sea bathing and forbid it altogether on certain days of the year. If you had to pay anyway, why not pay and swim in the lido, which was probably cheaper and offered better swimming than the sea? Also, you would not lose out on the days when the sea was considered too rough. The swimming pool at Hastings and St Leonards even offered sea bathing from the pool. (You changed in the lido and swam in the sea!)

The lido reached its zenith of popularity in the thirties. There were few new lidos built after the war. Gradually tastes changed and poor attendance made the pools uneconomic to run. Many fell into disrepair and decay and were finally demolished. It is sad to note that few pools remain today, but those that do are well worth the visit and well worth preserving. As a symbol of the thirties, the lido stands supreme, symbolizing as it did unashamed modernity, fashionable chic, youthful healthy activity and the cult of sun worship. If sun worship was the cult of the thirties, then the lido surely was its temple.

9 Piers and Picture Palaces

The pier has been synonymous with the English seaside holiday ever since the 1850s. In the inter-war period, it was as popular as ever. Indeed the loss of a pier through a natural disaster was often sorely felt. A reporter writing for the *Bristol and West Evening Times* in January 1932 felt that Weston-super-Mare's popularity was being severely restricted since its pier pavilion burned down almost exactly two years previously. He urged the local council to hurry up and approve plans for a replacement. The Council's reluctance was contrasted unfavourably with the policy of Bournemouth's council. He felt that Bournemouth was able to provide all manner of entertainment for visitors. The implication was that Weston was losing business by not having a usable pier.

The entertainment offered by piers and pavilions was very diverse. The traditional pierrot shows were carried over from the late nineteenth century in some resorts right through to 1939. In spite of their name, the pierrots had their roots not in the pier pavilion but in French pantomime. The pierrots wore white costumes with ruffles, pom-poms and skull caps. Their act usually consisted of comic sketches and rather sad songs, after which a hat was passed around for contributions. In the twenties the pierrots were joined by that most quintessential form of seaside entertainment, the concert party. If this was not to your taste, you could see the 'serious' theatre on a pier. For nine months of the year, avoiding the 'high season', the Repertory Theatre put on many West End plays at Hastings' Pier Theatre. They opened in October 1932 with Noel Coward's *Hay Fever.*

All forms of music were popular entertainment at the pier pavilions of the inter-war period. All tastes, ranging from the classical to the light, were catered for. Llandudno Pier, for example, employed a young Malcolm Sargent to conduct its orchestra. Many resorts had full-time municipal orchestras based on the pier. In the summer, the programme tended to be light classical; in the winter months, it was more high-brow. Military bands were also highly popular in the summer months and many played in open-air bandstands, either on the pier, or near the pier entrance. One form of Edwardian entertainment that did not survive the First World War, however, was the German band.

The traditional slot machines were as popular as ever (**63**). By the thirties, the 'What the Butler Saw' type of magic lantern slide machines or mutoscopes had become a touch more racy. One-armed bandits started to appear in numbers and pinball had invaded our shores from America. The pinball machines often necessitated a new amusement arcade to be added to the pier. One other machine which is familiar to us today – the crane hovering over a glass container full of prizes which are always just out of reach – made its first appearance in the thirties.

63 A selection of slot machines similar to those which would have been found on most inter-war piers. (Steven Braggs)

Another modern practice that was just beginning in the early years of the twentieth century was to have a fun fair at the end of the pier. The new Pavilion at Weston-super-Mare was eventually opened in 1933 and contained this type of amusement. Weston's Birnbeck Island Pier had been providing similar entertainment for years before.

Birnbeck or Old Pier (**colour plate 22**) was built around 1862. Unlike the majority of piers, it is actually a walkway out to an island. By the early twenties it boasted a variety of fairground-style attractions. These included a water chute, a switchback railway and a maze. There was also a pavilion with refreshments for sale and many other sideshows and amusements. Birnbeck Pier also fulfilled the traditional function of a pier, being a jetty for pleasure steamers. Visitors could choose between a number of different excursions to Cardiff, Newport, Barry, Bristol, Clevedon, Ilfracombe and Clovelly.

Yet another form of entertainment that could be found on the pier was dancing. It was highly popular throughout the inter-war period, perhaps only second to the cinema for popular recreation. Many piers played host to the Charleston and the Black Bottom in the twenties and in the thirties it was quite common to see the words 'OPEN-AIR DANCING' lit up in neon on many piers. Indeed, the holiday atmosphere often made people more inclined to participate than in their home towns.

Having established how popular the pier was in the inter-war years, it might seem rather surprising that there were no completely new piers built in this era. All construction work carried out on piers in the inter-war period was to repair damage to existing structures. One reason may have been that some of the pier projects started in the

Victorian age proved far from profitable. The most likely reason, however, is that nearly every resort that wanted a pier already had one. The new resorts that were just beginning to attract holidaymakers on the Cornish coast were seen as being uniquely unsuitable, given their rough seas, for pier construction.

No fewer than ninety-eight piers were built between 1814 and 1910. The first piers were purely practical structures designed to allow boats to moor and passengers to board and disembark. One of the first piers, the Chain Pier at Brighton built in 1823 by Captain Samuel Brown, was designed just for that purpose. Until it was built, passengers using the Brighton to Dieppe packet had to be carried to the boats or ashore by stout local fellows known as longshoremen. The pier was constructed using the suspension principle. The deck was suspended from chains running between four sets of piles. Above each set were two hollow iron towers used to support the chains. These towers were designed to allow small shops to operate from their base, selling various goods to the passengers.

Residents and visitors to Brighton found it pleasant to stroll along the pier and look out to sea in quiet contemplation, whether they were going to board a vessel or not. From then onwards the pier took on a second purpose, one of pure pleasure. Its association with sailing vessels and later paddle steamers, however, remained strong and most piers of the Victorian age were built with both aims in mind. Indeed through the twenties and thirties, paddle steamers offered holidaymakers the chance to take pleasure trips and excursions from the pier head, and the trade continued right up to the sixties.

Towards the end of the Victorian period, piers were being built not only as promenades and landing stations for pleasure boats and ferries, but with bandstands, theatres and pavilions as well. In many cases, these buildings were added to existing piers built originally with facilities that were more Spartan. It was in this period that the pier took on the form most associated with it today. The simple, functional styles of the first piers gave way to the oriental influence of the Brighton Pavilion.

One of the finest piers of the Victorian age was also at Brighton: the West Pier. It was designed by the engineer, Eugenius Birch, one of the most prolific pier builders of the age. When the pier opened in 1863, it had eight octagonal kiosks, but no other buildings. Promenaders were provided with seats along the pier and a windbreak along its centre. It was decorated in the classic Victorian style, with extensive use of wrought ironwork depicting images of snakes and dragons. In 1893, a theatre was built at the pier head and in 1916, a concert hall was added in the centre of the pier. The West Pier was still going strong in the thirties. The concert hall hosted performances by military bands in the summer and orchestras out of season. Other attractions included an 'Auto-Motor Track', 'Sunshine Shelters', bathing facilities and fishing.

Piers by their nature are precarious. They are at risk from the destructive power of the sea in rough weather and their wooden structure makes them vulnerable to fire. It was also not unheard of for piers to be damaged in collisions with ships.

Morecambe's pier was given a complete facelift using curved white concrete in 1936, after a fire the previous year. It now fitted in very well with the Midland Hotel and Super Swimming Stadium. Worthing's Pier, originally built in 1862, was bought by the local council in 1920 at a cost of £18,978. In 1925/26, it was given a new pavilion at the shore end (**64**), designed by architect, S.D. Adshead. A restrained form of Edwardian seaside style was used. It comprised a circular entrance hall with a main building behind. The whole structure has a most pleasing feel of simple elegance to it. In complete contrast, the seaward end was reconstructed after a fire between 1935 and 1937 using the latest modern style (**65, 66**). There is a curved amusement arcade, centrally placed in white, decorated with brown horizontal lines and a delightful Art Deco clock. A windbreaker in similarly decorated style runs the whole length to a pavilion at the far end, which is a round structure with a nautical feel to it. It is completely over the top, but in the best tradition of seaside building. Somehow, the two opposing styles seem to sit quite well together.

The pier head at Worthing was used to stunning effect in the recent (April 2000) television play *Cor Blimey!* about the off-screen affair between *Carry On* stars Sid James and Barbara Windsor. A ring of bikini-clad girls stood around the cylindrical pavilion representing the set of the film *Carry On Girls* (1973). The original film was about a beauty contest staged at the mythical resort of 'Fircombe'. In the original film, the West Pier at Brighton was used, but sadly, it is in no fit state for use today. It was closed in 1975 and has not opened since. It is no longer connected to the shore and is decaying into the sea. However, thanks to a grant from the National Lottery, the West Pier will now be saved.

Many piers were 'jazzed up' for the thirties. Hastings and St Leonards, an area keen to boost its popularity through modern architecture, provides two examples. Hastings Pier was given an Art Deco façade. It is an unusual structure, probably influenced by Ancient Egypt (**67**). St Leonards Pier, renamed the New Palace Pier, was given an even more brash appearance when a modernist metal and plaster entrance was added on the shore end.

64 Five views of the changing face of the British seaside between the wars. Here: Worthing Pier, shoreward pavilion, built in 1925 in traditional seaside style. (Steven Braggs)

Also at Worthing pier: the amusement arcade (built 1937, above, 65) and the seaward pavilion (built 1936, below, 66) in a modern style with a nautical flavour. (Steven Braggs (both))

67 The Art Deco façade on Hastings pier, built 1930. (Steven Braggs)

68 The rebuilt pier at Weston-super-Mare (built 1933). Note how the wrought iron work in the centre of the walkway contrasts with the Art Deco style of the pavilion beyond. (Diane Harris)

The British pier at night. Electric light was still relatively new in the thirties, and this made a wonderful subject for a postcard. Above (69) is Bournemouth around 1930 and below (70) is the Palace Pier, Brighton. Note the advertisement for open-air dancing at the entrance and the two charabancs on the front.

By night, the pier was (and still is today) a glorious display of coloured lights (**69, 70**). Electric light was still quite novel in the thirties and this was a marvellous subject for a picture postcard. It epitomised the atmosphere of the seaside town at night: Britain at play.

A rival to the bright lights and slot machines of the pier was the seaside cinema. The cinema reached the peak of its popularity in the early thirties, just after the talkies first appeared. Indeed, it was probably the most popular recreation activity of the thirties. While on holiday people expected to find the same type of entertainment as they had at home. By the thirties most towns had at least one cinema and probably more.

The cinema as a form of entertainment was well suited to the seaside. Most holidaymakers were in a mood to maximize the entertainment value of their one or two weeks by the sea. In fact, most seaside landladies' policy of insisting that guests be off the premises after breakfast and not return until after nine in the evening ensured, particularly on rainy days, a constant level of business for cinema owners (see Chapter 10). Most seaside holiday resorts were well provided for: for example, in 1934 Brighton had no fewer than sixteen cinemas; Bournemouth also attained that number by 1939. The major resorts were eager to point out that the latest films showing in London could be enjoyed at the seaside at a greatly reduced cost.

Like the pier, the cinema was designed to create a fantasy world. It gave ordinary people the opportunity to escape from their day-to-day concerns for a few hours and experience the magic of Hollywood. Indeed a number of the popular films of the day were about the glamour of show business itself. Cinema architecture reflected the glamour of this fantasy world. The very newness of the cinema as a form of entertainment meant that large numbers of cinemas were being built. Cinema design at the time went through a number of stylistic fads. First there was the Classical, then the Egyptian, then Art Deco, a brief flirtation with Spanish and finally the modern.

The style was often out of place in mock-Tudor suburbia, but was eminently suited to the seaside, where exaggeration and novelty had always been in vogue. The Odeon, with its familiar cream-tiled, flat-roofed towers, became a common sight at seaside towns (**71, 72**). Other cinema chains such as ABC found their way to the sea, following the suburban middle classes on their holidays. Many smaller independent cinemas also opened at the seaside (**73, 74**).

One of the first and most outstanding of all modern cinema designs is to be found at Dreamland in Margate. Dreamland was far more than a cinema. It was a gateway to a whole fantasy world comprising a cinema, an amusement park and a number of other attractions.

Dreamland's history goes back as far as 1867 when a disused Chatham and Dover Railway booking hall was converted into the Hall-by-the-Sea. It was used for concerts and other musical events. Seven years later 'Lord' George Sanger, a showman and circus owner from Tottenham in London, bought the site. He opened a menagerie and continued to stage concerts and dances. In 1893, a roller-skating rink was added. In 1905, the menagerie was closed and an amusement park opened for the first time on the site. Sanger sold the complex to John Henry Iles in 1915. In December 1919 the Hall-by-the-Sea was renamed the Palais de Dance. The following April it became Dreamland Hall and finally just Dreamland.

71 The cinema, as a building type, had its golden age in the thirties. It was as well represented at the seaside as in the major towns and cities. This is the Odeon, Blackpool, showing the familiar house style of the Odeon chain. (Diane Harris)

72 The Odeon, Weston-super-Mare, from a contemporary postcard. The film showing is The Scarlet Pimpernel, *starring Leslie Howard and Merle Oberon, which first opened in 1934.*

73 The Luxor Cinema, Eastbourne, which opened in 1933. It has now gone the way of many classic inter-war cinemas and become a bingo hall. (Steven Braggs)

74 The Plaza, Worthing, also opened in 1933. (Diane Harris)

75 The entrance to the Dreamland Amusement Park and cinema at Margate, built in 1935. It was the first building in England to use the finned tower format so often seen in cinema design. (Diane Harris)

Like the amusements at Blackpool's pleasure beach, Dreamland went through a number of facelifts throughout the twenties and thirties. In 1923, the Dreamland Super Variety Theatre was opened. It was built in Edwardian style. Later the original ballroom was revamped with mock-Tudor styling. One of the most popular amusement rides, the 'River Caves', was added in the mid-twenties.

The catalyst to redevelop the site came in 1930, when a fire destroyed the amusement park. Architects Leathart and Cranger were chosen to redesign the site. This partnership had already established a distinguished track record in the design of buildings for the entertainment industry. By this time, they had already designed four cinemas in London

76 The foyer of Dreamland. Note the pendant hanging from the ceiling and the geometric pattern around the central balcony. (Steven Braggs)

and the surrounding counties. They had used a variety of styles in their earlier work including Classical and Spanish.

Dreamland was to be built in an uncompromisingly modern style. The first part of the building to be opened was the front entrance (**75**) and café. It had to serve as an advertisement for the amusement park behind and attract visitors inside. The building was designed in a style as yet unseen in British cinemas and much followed by cinema architects ever since. A large tower in the form of a giant fin dominates the building. Running from the top to the bottom of the fin are the letters 'DREAMLAND'. To the left of the fin, looking at Dreamland from the front, is another smaller tower with space for advertising films and other attractions. It was a feature lacking in cinema design before Dreamland: in the past, very little consideration was given to space for displaying the current and forthcoming films. To the right of the tower is a large glass-fronted area. The whole structure is built of brick and must have looked very striking and modern. It is still standing, relatively unchanged from when it was first built.

The original Dreamland building, like contemporary public houses, had a public and a saloon bar. There was a café seating 300 people and·a restaurant seating 500. The cinema opened in 1935, attached to the entrance and café. It had a capacity of 2,000. The interior of the cinema was as opulent as the exterior was modern. Extensive use was made of different types of marble and handrails were in bronze. Careful consideration was given to the use of colour in the interior and the auditorium. Above the booking foyer is a circular balcony (**76**). Looking up at it, one can see a geometric pattern surrounding the balcony following its circular outline. A large pendant hangs down from the ceiling, many feet above the balcony. The auditorium itself, like many contemporary Odeons, was equipped with a Wurlitzer organ. The organ is illuminated and changes colour from blue to pink.

Margate's Dreamland was really the Londoners' equivalent of Blackpool's pleasure beach. It is interesting to note that Dreamland 'went modern' at around the same time as Emberton transformed the Pleasure Beach.

The style of the cinema influenced other seaside buildings of the pleasure industry. Theatre design also followed to a lesser extent some of the styling fads of the cinema industry. A good example is the Connaught at Worthing (**colour plate 23**). The Connaught was actually converted from the Picturedrome Cinema in 1935, although its modern and stylish façade was part of the conversion and not a carry over from the original cinema. The new theatre opened with a performance of *Theatre Royal* by Edna Ferber and George Kaufman on 30 September 1935.

The pier continues to be popular at the seaside, although a night-club or a greatly expanded arcade has often superseded the theatre and ballroom. The seaside cinema continues to be popular, although a large number of the thirties buildings are no longer used for their original purpose. Many have been converted into bingo halls (**73**).

10 Separate Tables

By the thirties, the really 'Grand Hotels' had had their day. They belonged to a different age. Their clients, who would have brought their servants with them, the very wealthy amongst the middle classes, were now holidaying abroad. Even as early as 1913, the manager of the Grand at Brighton was predicting a gloomy and unprofitable future. These hotels did enjoy a brief spell of profitability immediately following the First World War by offering luxurious living to the newly rich armaments makers and scrap metal dealers, but the increasing cost of labour made pre-war standards of comfort out of reach even to them.

The appeal of this type of hotel was limited to the older generation looking primarily for comfort rather than entertainment – the Grand's 1934 advertisement describes it as 'Brighton's most comfortable hotel'. In spite of the plight of the Grand Hotel, however, many slightly smaller Edwardian hotels continued to prosper in the expanding holiday market. Standards at these hotels were only slightly below those offered by the Grand Hotel; the main distinction was that these smaller hotels were never built to accommodate servants as well as guests. The thirties brought a brash new competitor appealing to those among the 'bright young things' who chose to spend at least part of their vacation in England – the modern hotel.

A select few strikingly modern hotels began to dot the English coast. Their number was limited, partly because many of the wealthy holidayed abroad, partly because many people still preferred traditional styles or even a combination of modern and traditional ideas, but mainly because hotel building had occurred at such a pace in earlier years that most resorts were already adequately served.

One of the first of these new buildings, the Midland, was built at Morecambe Bay for the LMS Railway to a design by Oliver Hill in 1933 (**77, 78**). The name 'Midland' was carried over from the original Midland Hotel, which was demolished to make way for the new one and is derived from its original owners, the Midland Railway. Hill's design was a curved structure, following the line of the coast, convex on the seaward side and concave on the shoreward side. The hotel had three storeys. The landward side was dominated by a large, circular central staircase, illuminated at night through double-glazed panels. The staircase was enclosed in a circular tower, at the top of which was a solarium for sunbathing. At the top of the tower are two stone seahorses by sculptor Eric Gill.

In spite of its monolithic concrete appearance, the building was in fact mainly constructed in brick, rendered with a material called 'snowcrete', comprising white cement and carborundum. The surface of the building was polished to a high degree of finish and the main window surrounds were bordered with a mixture of crushed blue glass and carborundum. At night the building was floodlit by concealed lighting and must have looked magnificent.

The Midland Hotel, Morecambe, as it was between the wars (77, above) and seen in 1996 (78, below). (Diane Harris)

Hill's work was well received in the press at the time. Several positive articles appeared in professional architectural journals. Much was made of the newness of the style and comparisons were made to similar modern buildings in Germany. Hill was an architect who did not pursue modernism as a theory, unlike many of his contemporaries, but regarded it merely as a style, which could be used if desired by the client. He exploited both the neo-Georgian and mock-Tudor styles that were popular at the time, as well as the modern. *Country Life*, a magazine not noted for its avant-garde following, was very complimentary about the Midland, although in general they preferred Hill's neo-Georgian buildings to his modern style ones.

Inside, the hotel was every bit as well designed as its exterior promised. Hill not only commissioned some of the most respected modern artists, but also took personal responsibility for the design of all the interior fittings. On walking through the revolving doors in the main entrance, underneath the circular staircase to the left one saw a stone relief by Eric Gill, depicting Nausicaa welcoming Odysseus, representing hospitality. (Gill's original design for the relief in the hotel, 'High Jinks in Paradise' depicting two nude couples and a nude woman, was rejected by LMS.) To the right was a polished aluminium glazed grill forming the entrance to the dining room. The floor was of polished marble inlaid with a mosaic pattern representing the ripples of the sea, together with the seahorse emblem. It was furnished with curved chairs designed by Hill and beautiful Art Deco rugs by Marion Dorn. The whole effect combined with the polished rail of the circular staircase was very modern and sophisticated.

The involvement of leading artists did not stop with the entrance hall. Gill also carved a medallion at the top of the staircase, inscribed with a line from Wordsworth: 'And hear old Triton blow his wreathed horn' (**colour plate 24**). It was painted by Dennis Tegetmeier. Edward Bowden designed a fresco in the children's room and a pictorial map of the district showing Morecambe's position and access to the Lake District and surrounding industry. Eric Ravilious painted a continuous mural of morning, noon and night, depicting life at Morecambe, for the café.

This café, which occupied the right-hand corner of the Hotel looking seaward, was circular in shape, with a full semicircle glazed facing the sea and the other semicircle displaying the mural. It was designed to be used by bathers at the Super Swimming Stadium, which was planned to open in the near future. Even if you could not afford to stay at the hotel, you could still appreciate its style and sophistication by having a cup of tea at the café.

The Midland was furnished exquisitely using only the finest materials. Weathered sycamore was used for the hall furnishings; white bur ash was used for the panelling on the outer walls of the dining room and for the chairs, and Nigerian cherry was used for the bedroom furniture.

The hotel was aimed squarely at the top end of the market. In an application for extended licensing hours, the hotel manager assured magistrates that the price of a ticket for its dinner dances at 8s 6d would exclude any undesirable types.

There was no real pattern to the location of these hotels. Those young and mobile with a new car and time and money on their hands could have chosen to go anywhere. There were modern hotels in the North, in the form of the Manchester in Blackpool, the Ship

A selection of the few modern hotels that started to dot the country in the thirties. 79, above: the Cumberland Hotel, Bournemouth. 80, overleaf top: the Beach Hotel, Worthing. 81, overleaf middle: the Ocean Hotel, Saltdean. 82, overleaf bottom: the Broadmark Hotel at Rustington in Sussex. (79-81: Diane Harris)

at Skegness and the Midland at Morecambe; in the West Country, represented by the St Austell Bay Hotel in Cornwall and Burgh Island Hotel, Bigbury Bay; and on the South Coast, such as the Beach at Worthing (**80**) and the Ocean at Saltdean (**81**). At the Ocean, it was not unknown for guests, wearing black tie and ball dresses, to punt across the hotel's swimming pool at midnight.

W.G. McMinnies, the author of *Signpost*, one of the first UK hotel guides and still going strong today, liked the Midland. He was, though, surprised to find it at Morecambe, 'a place chiefly famed for its shrimps and sand'[1]. He recommended it to those motoring up

PALACE COURT HOTEL

(Street Plan : Square J6)

Palace Court, Bournemouth's loveliest and most comfortable Hotel

In the heart of the colourful life of Bournemouth and facing the Pavilion, Gardens, Sun and Sea.

EVERY bedroom with bathroom and toilet, bedside telephone, writing desk and lounge furniture, making every room a suite. Many rooms with private sun-trap balconies overlooking the Bay.

Bridge organised every day by the Social Hostess.

Dancing to the Palace Court Hotel Band.

Membership of Palace Court Club with its cocktail bar available to visitors.

Direct access from the foyer to a hairdresser, costumier, outfitter, etc. Palace Court Theatre, the Ice Rink, two cinemas and many fashionable shops approachable under cover.

Golf, riding, yachting and tennis easily available. Sea bathing direct from the Hotel.

To more and more people a visit to Bournemouth means "Palace Court, of course." The increase in the number of visitors since the Hotel opened prove its magnetic appeal.

Jan.-Oct., 1936	...	...	6,524	visitors
Jan.-Oct., 1937	...	...	12,641	,,
Jan.-Oct., 1938	...	...	20,800	,,

These visitors include international stars of the stage and screen and celebrities in the literary and sporting world. Our folder, "A Word about Ourselves," issued monthly, tells about them. Write for the current Folder and the Hotel Brochure.

INCLUSIVE TERMS from Five Guineas a Week

REX GRUNDY, the Manager

SQUASH COURT

DANCING

BRIDGE

TABLE TENNIS

FULL
ENTERTAINMENT
PROGRAMME

FIREPROOF
BUILDING

TWO NIGHT
PORTERS

TWO PASSENGER
LIFTS

GARAGE ADJOINING

PALACE COURT HOTEL, BOURNEMOUTH

'*Phone* (*every room*) : Bournemouth 7100

Wires : Palcourt, Bournemouth.

83 'In the heart of the colourful life of Bournemouth', the Palace Court Hotel epitomizes thirties chic. (Bournemouth Tourism)

to Scotland or the Lake District as a good place to stop on the way. The appeal of this style of hotel to the young and fashionable was undoubted. W. G McMinnies, when describing the St Austell Bay Hotel in Cornwall, informs us that 'in the summer the unique sporting facilities it offers bring down scores of young and merry people'[1].

Both *Signpost* and the other well known motorists' touring guide to hotels, Ashley Courtenay's *Let's Halt a While*, began in the thirties. Ashley Courtenay included both the Beach Hotel at Worthing and the Ocean Hotel at Saltdean in his 1939 edition of *Let's Halt a While in and Around Kent, Surrey and Sussex*. He was impressed by the luxury of the Ocean and the range of entertainment that was on offer to guests. At the Beach, he liked the friendly atmosphere as well as the wide windows that let in the sunlight.

Bournemouth had two modern hotels, the Cumberland (**79**) and the Palace Court (**83**). The Cumberland was like an Aztec temple – a stepped pyramid in true Art Deco style. The Palace Court represented an interesting departure in hotel design. It was nine storeys high and as well as the main public rooms of the hotel, shops were provided on the ground floor. The upper storeys were designed as self-contained, serviced flats.

The Palace Court was built in 1936 in white concrete 'liner' style, with wrap-round curved 'suntrap' balconies although, like the Midland, the exterior was of rendered brickwork. This hotel, with its palmed garden, modern lounges and balconies laid for afternoon tea, was the epitome of thirties sophistication. At five guineas for a week, comparable with the Grand in Brighton, it was exclusive. An advertisement in Bournemouth's 1939 Guide describes it as being 'in the heart of the colourful life of Bournemouth' and describes the hotel's extensive facilities:

> Bridge organised every day by the Social Hostess.
> Dancing to the Palace Court Hotel Band.
> Membership of the Palace Court Club with its cocktail bar available to visitors.
> Direct access from the foyer to a hairdresser, costumier, outfitter, etc. Palace Court Theatre, the Ice Rink, two cinemas and many fashionable shops approachable under cover.[2]

One can easily imagine stylish living at this hotel in the thirties: a pre-dinner cocktail at the Palace Court Club; dinner, of course, would have been black tie; dancing to the hotel's own band; a rubber or two of bridge; and a last cocktail and cigarette before retiring to bed – it was another world!

These hotels had nothing in common with their Victorian and Edwardian predecessors. They were entirely of their own time, eminently appropriate for the age of the aeroplane

---

[1] *Signpost to Road Houses, Country Clubs and better and brighter Inns and Hotels of England* by W.G. McMinnies published by Simpkin Marshall Ltd 1935, by permission of Priory Publications Ltd, PO Box 24, Brackley, Northamptonshire NN13 5BR (the current publishers of *Signpost*).

[2] *The Book of Bournemouth – Britain's All-Seasons Resort Official Guide 1939-40* by permission of Bournemouth Tourism.

84 Art Deco detailing on a Regency-style hotel at Eastbourne. The straight lines of the hotel suit the Art Deco clock well; it would look less at home on a late Victorian building. Updating in this way was quite common. (Steven Braggs)

and the radio, and thoroughly up-to-date without a hint of revivalism. The style of the small, select groups of modern hotels encouraged many older hotels to update their appearance. Occasionally, Art Deco details such as clocks and other decoration can be seen on Regency and Victorian buildings (**84**) as well as complete refurbishment of the interior. Osbert Lancaster poked fun at this trend in *Progress at Pelvis Bay*:

> So great ... is the pace of modern life that in a few years the management, in pursuance of their well-known policy of always keeping abreast of the times, ... called in a well-known firm of Mayfair decorators to transform the hotel. The keynote of the scheme of decoration adopted was that of a ship, and every effort was made to emphasise this nautical idea in all the details of furnishing, with such successful results that the illusion of being on shipboard is almost complete and only slightly impaired by the uninterrupted view of the sea obtainable from most of the windows; were it invisible there would be nothing to indicate that one was not on the most modern of transatlantic liners.[3]

[3] *Progress at Pelvis Bay* by Osbert Lancaster, first published 1936 by John Murray, by permission of John Murray (Publishers) Ltd.

One relic from the Edwardian era that remained was the palm court, where guests and non-residents alike could take morning coffee or afternoon tea while listening to the latest music played by the hotel's resident orchestra (**85**). In Edwardian days, the favoured tunes would have been classical; in the twenties, jazz in the form of the Charleston and Black Bottom found its way to the seaside, following the night-club goers from London. By the thirties, the dance music mellowed into slower rhythms. The tea dance, or *thé-dansant*, was a regular feature of hotel life in the twenties and thirties. This gave non-residents an opportunity to sample the delights of more sophisticated hotels than their purse would allow and was a marvellous opportunity for middle-class boys and girls to meet on the dance floor.

The cocktail had also made its mark at the seaside, with many hotels having cocktail or 'American' bars. Another feature in demand was the sun lounge often with 'Vita' glass to let in the maximum amount of the sun's health-giving rays. The refurbishment programmes of many older hotels included the addition of a sun lounge in a modern style.

Most holidaymakers in the thirties would not have stayed in what then would have been called a 'swank hotel', but at one of the many medium-sized hotels, private hotels or boarding-houses that proliferated at the seaside resorts. Osbert Lancaster is more complimentary about this type of accommodation in describing the fictitious 'Balmoral' in *Progress at Pelvis Bay*:

> Erected in the middle of the last century, this charming building has been ever since a high-class private hotel. Though nowadays it may appear a trifle old-fashioned to some people, the façade has a distinct character of its own. The

85 Torbay Hotel is typical of a grand hotel of the early twentieth century, with palm trees and classical columns.

86 A classic hotel scene from the mid to late thirties. There is a fine selection of vintage cars parked outside a typical Blackpool hotel, only recently updated with a modern sun lounge.

interior, while retaining its old-world dignity and restraint as regards decoration, was modernised shortly before the war when bathrooms and gas lighting were installed. Among its faithful clientele are many who have come year after year since the hotel first opened its doors.[3]

It is this type of hotel, along with the boarding-house accommodation, that formed the backbone of the English seaside holiday throughout the inter-war period. It was not as stylish as the modernistic hotel, but it was adequate for its purpose. Visitors often returned time and time again to the same hotel. Advertisements from contemporary guidebooks provide a rich source of information on the feel of this kind of hotel at the time.

A few hotels in each resort firmly pitched for the business of the young. The Cliff House Hotel in St Leonards used a modern-style advertisement in the form of a flag pole with a large flag at the top displaying the hotel's name and a series of small flags describing the main features: 'Five Minutes New Bathing Pool; Garage; Dances, Whist Drives, Concerts and Tennis Drives; Young Society Catered For; Terms from $2\frac{1}{2}$ guineas per week.' Arnold House in Brighton sounded a similar refrain:

Jolly House. Near Sea and Pier. Young Society. Sports, Picnics, Bathing Parties. Large Garden. Croquet. Garage. Nine-hole golf, ping-pong, dancing,

[3] *Progress at Pelvis Bay* by Osbert Lancaster, first published 1936 by John Murray, by permission of John Murray (Publishers) Ltd.

music and songs, cards, whist drives, wireless. Morning excursions with guide. Trips to France.

It all sounds jolly good fun, indeed! Although there was less of a generation gap in the inter-war years, older people in search of the 'quiet luxurious comfort' offered by hotels such as the Royal Victoria in St Leonards, would have stayed well clear of these hotels.

Some hotels conversely sought to appeal to the old, particularly those who still came to the seaside under doctor's orders. But in the main, no section of the holiday market was particularly targeted by the advertising; most hotels sought to appeal to all. Referring to continental resorts, particularly the Riviera, in hotel advertising was also common.

Standards in hotel advertising improved in the mid to late thirties, as modern lettering was used **(87)** and attempts made to create an image for the hotel, rather than merely detailing its features and proximity to the coast and amenities. Some even went over the top in proclaiming its modernity, including pictures of aeroplanes flying overhead **(88)**.

87 Modern illustrations and lettering improved the standard of late-thirties hotel advertising. This is an example from Weston-super-Mare. (North Somerset Council and the Royal Grosvenor Hotel)

88 This advertisement for the Adelphi Hotel at Hastings is self-consciously modern with the appearance of an aeroplane buzzing overhead. (Hastings Borough Council)

ADELPHI

HOTEL

ST. LEONARDS-ON-SEA
(LICENSED)

Adjoining Promenade.   3 minutes Warrior Square Station
100 Rooms.   H. & C. Water throughout.   Electric Lift.   Central
Heating. Ballroom. Billiards. Table Tennis. Library. Night
Porter. Private Suites. Large Reception Rooms for Dinners,
                    Dances, Weddings, etc.
A.A.   R.A.C.

TELEPHONE : HASTINGS 622

Inclusive Terms :

DAILY   .   .   .   from 11/6 (minimum 2 days)
WEEKLY .   .   .   .   .   . from 3½ Guineas
Brochure on Application.   *Please mention this Guide*

GARAGE FOR 30 CARS ON HOTEL PREMISES

Usually high on the hoteliers' list of desirable features was proximity to the beach and amusements; phrases such as 'finest position on the sea front between the Palace and West Piers', 'central for all amusements', 'overlooking sea' and 'nearest licensed hotel to golf course and tennis' frequently appeared in advertisements. A sea view, particularly in hotels with balconies overlooking the sea, often commanded a premium in prices.

A study of advertisements placed in Bournemouth's 1939 Guide shows that by the end of the thirties, modern levels of comfort were beginning to appear. To give a fair comparison, the study was restricted to hotels with more than twenty-five rooms, or at least those that appeared to have at least that number where no figure was specified. Hot and cold running water in the bedrooms was mentioned in 80 per cent of the sample, but en-suite bathrooms were a much more recent innovation – only 6 per cent of hotels offered private bathrooms. 72 per cent offered gas or electric fires and 55 per cent had central heating. By this time the electric light was taken for granted, although earlier in the decade some advertisements still did refer to it. Beach huts exclusive to hotel guests were mentioned in 20 per cent of the sample. One interesting feature is that garages for guests were offered by 57 per cent of hotels and some even mentioned chauffeurs' accommodation. Garages are almost unknown today – when most people arrived by train at their holiday destination, hotels were able to pander to the minority of motorists. Another is the reference to separate tables for dining – these had been commonplace from the twenties onwards – but 29 per cent of hotels sampled still felt a need to refer to them. There must still have been hotels where a communal bench for all guests was provided for meals.

Hotels were keen to stress the modernity of their accommodation, phrases such as 'Recently entirely reconstructed, redecorated and refurbished' and 'Every modern convenience' were common. Also, references to electric power were frequent, with many advertisements mentioning 'electric lift'. AA classifications were just beginning but some hotels advertised themselves as 'AA and RAC appointed'. Few stated the actual classification unless it was five star. Entertainment and sports facilities usually featured

89 The delightful Art Deco lounge of the Carlton Hotel at Lytham St Anne's. The decor of smaller hotels followed contemporary suburban fashion.

strongly: 'maple sprung ballroom', 'swimming pool', 'ping-pong' and 'tennis' were often mentioned. Tennis became highly popular in the thirties when Fred Perry triumphed at Wimbledon, and many hotels had their own courts.

Finally, the terms would be mentioned; prices were usually in guineas. Some hoteliers, not necessarily catering for the very top of the market, clearly felt the mention of money was too vulgar and simply stated 'moderate terms'. The package often included breakfast, lunch, dinner, afternoon tea and morning coffee as well. Clearly, hotel guests were not expected to stray far from the hotel.

There are also some unusual comments worth reproducing: 'No absurd restrictions' was a frequent comment. Some hotels in the twenties did not permit residents to take a bath after 10 p.m. and bathrooms were kept locked. The Linden Hall Hydro, Bournemouth, pandered to every conceivable health fad, offering: 'Medical treatments given by fully qualified attendants.... Foam bath. Studa chair. Artificial sunlight. Diathermy, ionisation, Faradism and all electrical treatments'. The owners of the Linga Longa Hotel, Bournemouth, must have felt self-conscious about not having a swimming pool: 'Bathing direct from the house, free of expense at any time... for that reason a swimming pool on the premises is superfluous'. However, the most unusual comment must surely be 'No Aspidistras' at the Tower House, Bournemouth!

The distinction between the guest house and the small private hotel is a very subtle one. The use of the title 'hotel' would appeal to those middle-class customers who would be prepared to spend an extra half-guinea a week in return for some 'snob value'. Advertisements usually stressed the quality of their cooking and the homeliness of the atmosphere. 'Under personal supervision of the proprietor' was the usual formula for small private hotels – if you cannot offer the grand and lavish, stress the personal touch. According to Anthony Hern in *The Seaside Holiday,* the presence or absence of servants assisting the landlady was a determining factor, as was the façade of the building – a double-fronted house could be called a hotel.

For the working man and his family, the most usual type of accommodation would have been the guest house. Before the First World War, landladies in Blackpool and other working-class destinations operated what was known as the 'Apartment System'. A whole house, a room, a shared bedroom or even a shared bed would be let to a visitor and his family. Usually the price of the accommodation would include the use of the lounge. The guest would supply his own food and the landlady would cook it. 'Extras', at extra cost, might include bread, milk, potatoes, hot water for tea and even use of the cruet set. Landladies would also wash guests' clothes and clean boots, again for extra cost.

This type of lodging was gradually replaced during the inter-war period with the 'Board System'. The landlady provided full board, usually including breakfast, lunch and dinner, for an inclusive weekly rate. The 'Apartments System', however, continued throughout the period, offering the cheapest type of accommodation to those who could only afford the bare minimum.

The two most common gripes and the subject of countless comic postcard jokes about boarding house accommodation were petty restrictions and overcrowding (**90**). Certainly some of the restrictions were born of trying to reconcile the needs of the more boisterous visitors with those who preferred peace and quiet and an early night. Blackpool's Hotel and Apartments Association, effectively the landladies' trade association, recommended that members did not allow piano playing after 11 p.m.

Other restrictions were mainly for the convenience of the landlady. Some establishments offering bed and breakfast only often turned guests out of their rooms at 10 a.m. and did not allow them back until 9 p.m., come rain or shine. It is fortunate that the resorts offered such a varied degree of entertainment and many cheap cafés and restaurants, including the ubiquitous fish and chip bars.

As for overcrowding, it is certainly true that in the more popular resorts, at the height of the season, it was not unknown for guests to be billeted in baths or on upturned tables – and these were the lucky ones. Those who did not book in advance, coming down 'on spec', could find themselves sleeping on the beach. Margaret Lockwood and Hugh Williams do just that in the 1938 film *Bank Holiday*, when they find the Grand Hotel full at the mythical resort of Bexborough.

Standards of lodging house accommodation rose during the inter-war period. Separate tables, running water in bedrooms (though not necessarily hot) and electric lights became more common, although by no means universal. Many landladies now saw fit to give their establishments the grander sounding title of 'private hotel'. Those back-street lodging homes offering the minimum standard hardly improved at all.

One form of accommodation that is not common today was the temperance hotel. Often on a large scale, these institutions offered hotel-style accommodation in

90 Overcrowding in hotels was a problem during the high season and on bank holidays. This postcard is by Tom Browne.

91 Modernistic temperance accommodation: Oulton Hall in Clacton-on-Sea offered hotel-style facilities at exceptional value.

unlicensed premises at considerably lower costs than contemporary hotels. One such example was Oulton Hall at Clacton-on-Sea (**91**). A smart, modern building, described as a 'Super Guest House', the hotel offered accommodation for 250 people in bedrooms with hot and cold running water. Features included 'Three dances weekly on Sprung Dance Floor. Lift. Sun Roof. Hard Tennis Courts. Billiards. Garage', all for the exceptional price of $2\frac{1}{2}$ guineas, little more than a small guesthouse.

Both the boarding house and the seaside hotel continued to flourish after the war, but standards were not the same, at least as far as the AA was concerned, as no hotels were awarded the five star classification again until 1955.

11 'Our True Intent is All for Your Delight'

Butlin's first holiday camp, opened in Skegness in 1936, was a phenomenal success, attracting some 10,000 enquiries from the initial half-page advertisement placed in the *Daily Express* which promised 'holidays with three meals a day and free entertainment from 35s to £3 per week according to season'.[1] The idea was so popular with the public that by the time the camp first opened its doors on Easter Saturday in 1936, it was already fully booked for the season.

Butlin's original idea came from dissatisfaction with the traditional boarding house accommodation that he had stayed in during his former career as a travelling showman:

> I felt sorry for myself, but I felt even sorrier for the families with young
> children as they trudged along wet and bedraggled, or forlornly filled in time
> in amusement arcades until they could return to the boarding houses.[1]

He compared the boarding house holiday to happier holidays he had spent in a camp in Canada, where he had formerly lived, and vowed that one day he would build a holiday camp. When he did, it was to be on a grand scale.

The Butlin's camp was a miniature seaside resort. It sought to create a fantasy world for its residents within its perimeter. That fantasy world was the one they had seen at the cinema and read about in popular magazines such as *Picture Goer*, which talked at length about the extravagant lifestyles of the movie stars, illustrated by numerous glossy pictures. What Butlin attempted to do was to allow his campers the opportunity to escape from their daily lives, not for a couple of hours at the cinema, but for a whole week.

As such, the Butlin's camps, both at Skegness and his second camp at Clacton-on-Sea, which opened in 1938, reflected this fantasy world. The main camp buildings were essentially modern in appearance. Functional white concrete blocks were used at Skegness (**92**), whereas the Clacton camp was fronted by a magnificent Art Deco façade in the stepped pyramid style (**93**). Both camps had outdoor swimming pools with cascades, the pool at Clacton being of an unusual L-shaped design.

Inside the camps' main buildings the same theme continued. Both camps had bars, large dining rooms and ballrooms, and their features were designed to create an atmosphere of luxury. The bar at Clacton was typically thirties and could have come from a 'Grand Hotel' or luxury liner (**94**). It had modern tubular steel furniture, a luxurious

---

[1] *The Billy Butlin Story: A Showman to the End* by Sir Billy Butlin, published by Robson Books, by permission of Robson Books.

92 Modernistic style in the swimming pools and main buildings of Skegness.

93 The Bathing Pool at Butlin's, Clacton-on-Sea. The main building is in the Art Deco stepped pyramid style. (Jarrold & Sons Ltd)

94 *Grand hotel or ocean liner? Only the presence of the Redcoats gives this smart bar away as Butlin's at Clacton-on-Sea. Billy Butlin tried hard to build a stylish image on a limited budget; note the palms, chrome plate and modern furniture.*

tiled interior, copious chrome plate and a uniformed doorman. The ballrooms and dining halls echoed the same style.

Paradoxically, however, the chalets in which the campers slept, although thoroughly up-to-date for the time with hot and cold running water, were built in 'traditional' mock-Tudor style, with exposed beams (**95**). It seems that on holiday, as well as at home, while people were quite happy to go into brash, modern buildings such as cinemas for entertainment, they still preferred to come back at night to their own little Tudor cottage – or at least Mr Butlin perceived that they did. The image of the camps, however, had to be built on a budget. Butlin needed to ensure that the holidays were reasonably priced. Consequently, the atmosphere of luxury was to a certain extent only skin deep.

The entertainment offered to the campers needed to reflect the opulent image that Mr Butlin wanted to create. His mass audiences were sufficient to attract the stars of radio, the cinema and the sporting world. Gracie Fields, Elsie and Doris Waters, Will Fry, Will Fyffe (from the popular radio show *Monday Night at Eight*), cricketer Len Hutton, Len Harvey (British light heavyweight boxing champion) who sparred with a kangaroo, and from the world of snooker Joe Davis, all entertained at Butlin's in the thirties. Dan Maskell gave tennis lessons and Victor Sylvester gave dancing lessons. Butlin's camps also had their own resident orchestras playing the dance hits of the era.

In addition to the major stars from the early days, the Butlin's Redcoats were always on hand to ensure that the campers got the most from their holidays. The idea for the Redcoats came to Butlin early on in the Skegness camp's first season. He saw the first campers walking around looking bored and not making full use of the facilities. They had come to the camp looking for companionship and were not finding it. One of his assistants, Norman Bradford, started to 'jolly up' proceedings by telling a few jokes to the campers assembled in the dining room. Butlin thought this was a good idea and the next day asked his colleague to go out and buy a distinctively coloured blazer – he did, in blue, primrose yellow and white, the camp colours. Butlin was not convinced and asked him instead to buy a red blazer. The Red Coats were then born. The famous 'hi-de-hi, ho-de-ho' routine also started in the thirties; Butlin borrowed the idea from an army routine in an American film, thus continuing the cinema link.

The atmosphere of the camps is captured in miniature by some of the badges issued to the campers, originally given out for identification to gain entrance to the camp. The badge issued for Clacton in 1938 featured a girl in swimsuit and bathing cap holding a champagne glass with the caption 'champagne air' (**96**). One lady camper told *Picture Post* that she saved up all year to have a champagne cocktail on every night of her holiday. Butlin's issued badges – a different design each year – right up to 1967.

In advertising the camps, Butlin teamed up with the LNER, who had an interest in promoting holidays on the East Coast. LNER actually paid for 50 per cent of all Butlin's advertising costs and Butlin's second camp at Clacton was opened on an LNER line. The Clacton Camp is illustrated by a delightful railway poster produced by LNER showing the swimming pool in the foreground and the main camp building bearing Butlin's famous motto: 'Our true intent is all for your delight'. Although this is a quotation from Shakespeare's *A Midsummer Night's Dream*, Butlin confessed in his autobiography, *The Billy*

THE CHALETS, BUTLIN'S HOLIDAY CAMP, SKEGNESS

95 Chalets at Butlin's, Skegness. Note the mock Tudor style with oak beams. This was in complete contrast to the modern style of the other buildings in the camp.

96 Champagne and swimming
pools – the spirit of Butlin's in
the thirties. One female camper
told a Picture Post reporter that
she had saved up all year so that
she could have a champagne
cocktail every day of her holiday.
The badges were issued to
campers every year up to 1967.
(Diane Harris)

Butlin Story, that he borrowed it from a fairground organ! This type of poster would have been seen in LNER trains and stations in the late thirties. Since train travel had only the motor bus to compete with for the majority of holidaymakers, this was a sure way of attracting customers to LNER.

The popularity of the camps increased further when the Government passed legislation giving all industrial workers a week's paid holiday in 1938. Butlin's advertisements proclaimed: 'Holidays with pay: Holidays with play: A week's holiday for a week's wage'.[1] By the end of the thirties, 15 million people in the UK had paid holidays.

However, in spite of this campaign, the majority of Butlin's campers were not drawn from the working classes, but were from the lower middle classes – often bank clerks and their wives. The cost of catering, even on a mass scale, was still too high for most working men, who still tended to go to the traditional boarding houses in the thirties.

As to what life in the camps was actually like, Tom Wintringham, writing for *Picture Post* in August 1939, felt that, paradoxically, camp life offered more freedom and privacy to the average holidaymaker in the thirties than the seaside landlady did. When comparing camping in general to that more traditional form of holiday accommodation, Mr Wintringham says:

[1] *The Billy Butlin Story: A Showman to the End* by Sir Billy Butlin, published by Robson Books, by permission of Robson Books.

The rain might creep in; but the landlady did not. Walls might let in draughts; but there were no neighbours close enough to tap on the wall if you snored. You were 'on your own'.[2]

His view is that this privacy was still present in a Butlin camp:

> The new form of holiday camp gives you this essential privacy in the shape of a hut or chalet made of concrete, timber and asbestos sheet roofing.... But added to this privacy, and not conflicting with it, the new sort of camping provides as much social life and as much play and pleasure as you can desire and can endure.[2]

In this last phrase, there is possibly a hint of cynicism, but 'endure' is more likely to be a mannerism rather than a criticism, as overall, Mr Wintringham is complimentary about camp life. The new camps were a classic thirties compromise: privacy and a full social life; modernity in the style of the buildings and the amenities, but homeliness in the mock Tudor style of the chalets.

The criticism levelled at the camps by commentators of the time and in later years was that of regimentation: that the camps made mass-produced leisure and compulsory fun and games. Working men, it was assumed, were used to regimentation in their day-to-day life working at factories – clocking in and out, following the rules. Commentators felt that Butlin's style of holiday provided the regimentation that they had become used to at work in their leisure as well. Tom Wintringham, however, still believed that the camps paradoxically gave campers more freedom, particularly those with limited resources:

> The ability to choose what you like without worrying over the cost of it... The bathing in sea or heated swimming pool, the tennis, the games to join in on the greens and the games to watch in the stadium, are all included in the $3\frac{1}{2}$ guineas each adult pays. The boating lake, darts, putting and bowling greens, and roller skating rink are all 'thrown in'. If others are waiting to play tennis, you can only have half an hour. But if no-one else is wanting your tennis court, you can play from 10 a.m. to nearly midnight. Courts are floodlit: games can go on till 'hostilities cease' at 11.45 p.m.[2]

This is all very true. The fact remained, though, that to anyone going on holiday in search of peace and quiet, the holiday camp would be the last place on Earth in which to find it. For those who revelled in the company of others, the holiday camp was the ideal place to go.

However, in spite of their size and publicity, Butlin's were by no means the only holiday camps in Britain between the wars. Camping as a form of leisure activity had began to become popular in the late Victorian era and the first holiday camp was the Cunningham

[2] From the article 'Holiday Camp' by Tom Wintringham, in *Picture Post*, 5 August 1939. Reproduced courtesy of IPC Magazines Ltd.

97 The true spirit of camping at a typical inter-war pioneer camp.

Camp for men only on the Isle of Man, opened in 1894. Campers at Cunningham's actually stayed in tents and conditions were basic. By the early twenties, a number of what became known as 'pioneer camps' (**97**) had opened, offering basic accommodation and a genuine camp atmosphere where holidaymakers joined in with the daily chores of running the camp. The idea of camping and life under canvas was well matched to the inter-war fad for healthy outdoor life. These camps soon became more permanent with canvas replaced by chalets and communal buildings for eating and entertainment. The early entrepreneurs were also joined by trade unions and the co-operative movement in the camp business, offering exclusive facilities to their members. The most well known of these was for members of NALGO (National and Local Government Officers' Association, now part of UNISON) and for civil servants.

The philosophy of these pioneer camps was completely at variance with that of Butlin's. The organizers and campers felt that their style of holiday was in tune with the true spirit of camping.

> What shall profit a camper if he gain the service of a Grand Hotel and lose the easy camaraderie which made a holiday camp so refreshingly different from anywhere else?[3]

[3] Taken from *Goodnight Campers! The History of the British Holiday Camp* by Colin Ward and Dennis Hardy, published by Mansell in 1986.

Butlin's by no means had the monopoly on the so-called 'mass camps' between the wars. The Prestatyn Holiday Camp, opened in 1939, was a joint venture between the LMS railway company and Thomas Cook. It boasted some excellent modern buildings, including the Prestatyn Clipper (98, above) and the Hamlyn Tower (99, below).

Since Butlin was trying to recreate the atmosphere of the Grand Hotel on a budget, this quotation shows just how far apart the two philosophies were.

W.J. Brown, the founder of the Civil Service Clerical Association's holiday camps at Corton and Hayling Island, held the view that camps should accommodate no more than 500 people. Beyond that number he considered that it was not possible for a 'very rich and full corporate life' to be enjoyed by the campers. Billy Butlin himself found this true when he noticed his very first campers appearing bored and introduced the Redcoats to stimulate this kind of atmosphere.

Butlin's did not have the monopoly over modern architecture at camps. One particularly fine example from the pioneer camps is Rogeston Hall at Corton, just North of Lowestoft in Suffolk. This camp was opened by the Workers' Travel Association and was intended to provide cheap holidays with a reasonable level of comfort to workers and their families. As with Butlin's, the camp had a modern main building, but its most unusual feature was that its chalets were built in unified blocks, rather than as separate units. This found favour with architectural critics at the time, possibly because it was replicating in miniature the conflict between semi-detached suburbia and the council estate.

Another strikingly modern camp was built jointly by Thomas Cook and LMS at Prestatyn and opened in 1939 (**98, 99**). It is possible that LMS executives felt LNER's link with Butlin's was losing them business. This camp went one stage further than Butlin's in recreating the atmosphere of the ocean liner – it actually had its own liner deck built on shore, complete with masts and flags, the 'Prestatyn Clipper'. The camp was built on the same scale as Butlin's with accommodation for 1,750 campers. The camp buildings were designed by William Hamlyn, architect for LMS. From the entrance between two rectangular shaped columns, between which was suspended the text 'Prestatyn Holiday Camp – The Chalet Village by the Sea', to the white concrete of the main buildings with flat roofs in typical functionalist style, to the swimming pool with its observation tower, the camp is classic thirties style. The 'Prestatyn Clipper' is possibly a little over the top and lacking in subtlety, compared with such buildings as Embassy Court at Brighton, which only suggests the ocean liner, rather than replicates it, but it must be remembered that this is a holiday camp where its visitors were permitted to indulge in fantasy for their short stay.

When the war came in 1939, it was a shock to Billy Butlin. He had confidently predicted that the crisis would blow over and was already planning his next camp at Filey, due to open in 1940. However, in true entrepreneurial spirit, he coped with the war when it came. Through a deal with the War Ministry, who took over his camps at Clacton and Skegness, he completed the Camp at Filey and built two other camps at Ayr and Pwllheli. He negotiated a scheme giving him the right to buy the camps back at the end of the war and at the close of hostilities, Butlin was left in a very strong position. His camps really came into their own in the fifties and became the epitome of the working man's holiday in that era. The pioneer camps fared less well and many never re-opened. For some, the true spirit of camp life was lost forever.

12 'Wish You Were Here'

On holiday, time is precious. This was especially true if you had only one week out of fifty-two away from the routine of day-to-day living. If you wanted to send a note to a friend, it was better to scribble a few words on the back of a postcard than to write a lengthy letter. Messages such as this one sent by one of the very first visitors to Butlin's camp at Clacton-on-Sea were typical:

> Having a lovely time. Weather OK. Will have heaps to tell you when I come home. Lots of love. Audrey.

The picture postcard is almost entirely a twentieth-century phenomenon. Before 1894, the Post Office would not accept postcards and up to 1902, the whole of the back of the card was used for the address. The message had to share the front of the card with the picture. Once these restrictions were lifted, there was an explosion in postcard design. Almost every conceivable seaside subject was photographed: piers, promenades, swimming pools, bathers, children, donkeys and ponies, views of the town and landscapes. Throughout the inter-war years, literally thousands of seaside pictures were commissioned from local photographers. Hotels and boarding houses often had their own cards, as a bit of free advertising, as did Butlin's and the other holiday camps.

It is interesting to note that a number of postcards we have come across from this era have not actually been sent. This suggests that they were bought as a souvenir of the holiday as well as to send to friends and relatives at home.

One particular form of the postcard, the comic card, flourished in the twenties and thirties. Donald McGill was the most prodigious exponent of this art. His cards were a caricature of the British public on holiday. In many respects, they were the perfect foils to the guidebooks and railway posters. The job of the guidebook and poster was, of course, to attract holidaymakers to the resorts. They portrayed an ideal of the English summer holiday. In this ideal, the sun was always bright, the skies were always blue and the sand was always golden. The people that lived in this ideal world were perfect too. Children were always smiling and enjoying themselves sailing boats or making sand castles. Ladies were always young and slim and wore the latest in fashions or swimming costumes. Men were young and sporting, suave and sophisticated, or the perfect father.

In the world of the comic postcard, life was different. There is a card of a grossly fat man relaxing on the beach, smoking a cigar and surrounded by empty beer bottles. It has the caption 'I'm thinking of swimming the Channel – but not this week!' (**colour plate 25**). Another shows a large young lady sporting a rather revealing (for the time) bathing

100 An early novelty postcard. The middle section opens up to reveal a long streamer printed with views of Bognor Regis. The passengers are wearing typical fashions of the early twenties.

costume with the caption 'My new bathing dress is quite a success – What you can't see of me of course you must guess!' (**colour plate 28**). There are three thin men looking on sniggering. The message on the back of the card is equally revealing:

> Dear Anne, I'm having a fine time here. the weather is glorious so far. We are just going to meet the boys. Cheerio Margaret.

She also adds as a postscript: 'That's me on the back'!

McGill's humour in these cards does show a slightly cruel streak. Another of his cards shows a tarty but far from attractive girl walking along the beach wearing pink beach pyjamas. She has a ludicrously dainty handbag and is smoking a cigarette. A young man in a striped blazer and grey flannels gives a mocking wolf whistle. The caption reads 'Just because I'm smart the men think I'm fast!' (**colour plate 29**).

Another line in McGill's cards appeals to the lad away on holiday sending a card back to his pals at home. One card shows two men walking along the promenade. One wears a trilby hat, a brown sports jacket and carries a cane. The other has the ubiquitous striped blazer and smokes a pipe. A young lady is in front of them. She is wearing a twenties style short skirt. The breeze from the sea is just strong enough to raise her skirt just enough to afford the young gentlemen behind her a view of her stocking tops. Both men register delight on their faces. The caption, which would be unacceptable today, reads 'It's better to be deaf than blind!' (**colour plate 26**).

The theme of young love is carried through in many of McGill's cards. One shows an open charabanc with a young couple sitting at the back. They stare dotingly into one another's eyes. The caption says 'I was coming all the way by Charabanc – but I "got off" before I reached here!' (**colour plate 27**). We assume a more innocent meaning to the phrase 'got off' than it would carry today!

For other tastes, some of McGill's cards exploit crude humour of a different kind. One card reads 'Of the "Bottomless Sea" the poets sing. But down here we've got quite a different thing'. The card depicts four large figures, two men and two women, wearing striped and spotted swimwear. Each of them of course is displaying a rather large rear end!

As well as showing us that the human body on holiday was a far from ideal sight, McGill and others also tell us that the holiday experience itself might not have been the ideal the guidebooks would have us believe. Travelling to the seaside by charabanc could hardly have been luxurious and was possibly even unsafe. But it was perhaps not as precarious as on the charabanc that McGill shows balancing just above a cliff edge. The caption reads 'We've stopped here – for the present'. Other cards show grotesquely overcrowded hotels and one even shows an upturned boat being used as a boarding house.

The seaside holiday was an excuse for indulgence and, more than likely, over-indulgence. A postcard by another artist has the caption: 'I've spent some jolly evenings round the bandstand' (**colour plate 30**). It shows a smartly dressed gentlemen, propping himself up against the bandstand. He is smoking a big cigar and has a walking cane – but his collar is halfway round his neck and his face has the warm red glow of an evening on the booze!

The world of the comic postcard was clearly an exaggerated one. You cannot imagine holidays were ever as bad as some cards depict. The world of the guidebooks and the posters was the ideal. The reality clearly lay somewhere between the two.

Time was precious in another way, too. If you had only a week to enjoy yourself, it was all the more important to record your holiday joys so as to relive them in the winter months and think of next year. Photography had been a popular hobby with the troops in the trenches in the First World War. They were able to record the war as it really was. The habit stuck and the camera was now used to catalogue more pleasurable memories.

In these early days of snapshot photography, people took far fewer photographs than most do today. Often a single hard-backed album would contain many years' worth of photographs. People took considerable time and trouble to place the photographs in the album and caption them carefully. The album would then provide a permanent record of the holiday experience for years to come.

Camera manufacturers recognized the annual holiday as a prime marketing theme, associating the camera with fun and sunshine. Most advertising of the time featured the use of a camera at the seaside. The camera most holidaymakers would have used was basic. The two most popular designs were the box camera or the folding camera. The folding camera was quite compact and looked more complex than the box camera. In fact, they were functionally very similar. Both were little different to the box cameras that Kodak popularized in the early 1900s. Kodak, in those days, reigned supreme in this market as a manufacturer of both film and cameras. Roll film (either 127 or 120) was the most widely used film format and holiday snaps were always black and white. Although colour film, the 35mm format and flash photography were available, they were either prohibitively expensive, excessively complex or both.

Snapshot cameras, inter-war style. The Beau Brownie (101, top) with Art Deco panel, was a basic box Brownie restyled by Walter Dorwin Teague. The Purma Special (102, below) was deigned by Raymond Loewy, but manufactured in England by R.F. Hunter. Although hardly typical of the run of cameras most people would have used, both were affordable and would have been used by holidaymakers. (Diane Harris)

In the 1920s Kodak aimed a lot of their advertisements and marketing strategy at female buyers. They believed that women were much more likely to use the camera all year round. Men by contrast were inclined to put it back in the cupboard until next year once the holiday was over. The fact that women were less likely to restrict the camera's use to holidays only was important to Kodak, whose main business was always the sale of film, rather than of cameras. This targeting of women as consumers had a profound effect on the style of cameras of the late 1920s and early 1930s.

Kodak enlisted the help of Walter Dorwin Teague, a well-known American industrial designer of the period, to style a range of coloured folding cameras aimed primarily at female buyers. They were known as 'Vanity Kodak' and were available in five colours, decorated with gold lines. The cameras were supplied in a matching case with a silk lining. Teague also transformed the basic Box Brownie by styling an Art Deco metal front panel, available in a wide range of colours. These cameras were known as 'Beau Brownies' (**101**). However, the most exciting design by Teague, for Kodak, of this coloured camera period, was a folding camera featuring a modern design of different, brightly coloured circles and squares, available with a matching case. The trend for coloured cameras came to an end after the early thirties, with black once more becoming the dominant colour.

Perhaps the most significant influence of 1930s style on camera design came with the advent of Bakelite. Initially, Bakelite was used to imitate styles already available. Kodak's No. 2 Hawkette, introduced in 1927, had a basic shape that was little different from the folding cameras already on the market. Manufacturers even produced replicas of the box design, right down to the sharp edges and corners, which were difficult to make in Bakelite. However, as with other applications of Bakelite, ideas that were more original soon came to the fore, making full use of its property of being easily moulded into different forms.

The basic snapshot camera was transformed in 1934, when Walter Dorwin Teague restyled the Brownie. A curved shape was used that was easy to hold and suited the manufacturing process for Bakelite. Vertical lines were used, which gave the camera its style, and there was a hint of streamlining. Streamlining was taken further by another great designer, Raymond Loewy, famous for his styling work for the Studebaker car company in the 1950s. He designed the British-made 'Purma Special' (**102**), the first snapshot camera to offer a fast shutter speed for action shots. The camera is a delight to use, even today. The controls are simple and easy to operate and cleverly integrated into its smooth Bakelite shape. The camera has a pop-out lens, reckoned to be of high quality at the time, which retracts when its lens cap is screwed on. This feature and its elegant black style give it the feel of a modern compact camera. As befitting a product of a leading designer, the 'Purma Special' is packed with innovative features, including a three-speed shutter, altered by gravity according to whether the camera is held horizontally or vertically. This had no effect on the orientation of the picture, as the square negatives were produced from the 127 film, enabling sixteen rather than eight pictures to be taken from one roll.

The snapshot camera would have brought pleasure to millions in this era and made a significant contribution to the family holiday. It became an essential ingredient of the annual holiday that is still with us today. The comic postcard has survived political correctness and is also just as much a part of the British seaside holiday now as it was then.

13 1939: The Last Season and Beyond

In the closing years of the thirties, there was a feeling of deepening crisis. It was as if the storm clouds were gathering ever darker. A study of the first issues of *Picture Post* (first published in 1938) shows an increasing interest in the threat from Germany. Among the more light-hearted articles about chorus girls, the snapshots of film stars and important public figures off duty, and the more serious articles about working men in all sorts of different occupations, are discussions of German air power, reviews of aspects of life in Nazi Germany and essays about the 'crisis' itself. Chamberlain's deal with Hitler in Munich had averted the immediate threat of war in 1938, but it had left an uneasy peace.

Even in the autumn of 1938, before the deal had been agreed, appeals were made over loudhailers to Britons at leisure, in the cinema, at the swimming gala and at social functions to go and have their gas masks fitted. In the months after Munich, Britain was preparing for war. Conscription was announced for men aged twenty and twenty-one in April 1939. Frantic provisions for rearmament were already under way and trenches had already been dug in London.

In spite of this, the mood among the public was still optimistic. It had been accepted that war was likely at some point, but at least not yet. The 1939 holiday season began as any other. The most contemporary account of inter-war life, *'The Long Week-end'* by R. Graves and A. Hodge, published in 1941, tells us of a cartoon from a current issue of *Punch* 'showing a well-dressed middle-class Suburbitonian furiously hurling a book at his Cassandra-like radio. The British should be allowed to take their summer holiday in peace'[1], and not be bothered by constant coverage by the media of the so called 'crisis'. *Picture Post* of the time shows us a picture of a bowler-hatted man sitting on Brighton beach studying a newspaper article titled 'My reply to Goebbels', but most of the other holidaymakers shown in the same article were enjoying themselves.

The holiday trade too, was optimistic. Billy Butlin believed right up to the last minute that war would be avoided, but this may have been blatant commercialism. When war finally was declared on 3 September 1939, most people at least had had the chance to have their last summer holiday of the thirties. Even after war was declared, many of the resort's local councils were still optimistic. Even resorts on the South Coast produced guidebooks for the 1940 summer season with the theme 'business as usual'.

---

(1) *The Long Week-end: A Social History of Great Britain 1918-1939* by R. Graves & A. Hodge, published in 1941 by the Readers' Union Ltd by arrangement with Faber and Faber Ltd.

The reality of the war for many seaside towns was very different. Many on the West Coast took in thousands of evacuees. Blackpool played host to the armies of Britain and the other allied powers throughout the conflict. The promenade became a drill ground, the dance halls were now gymnasiums.

Resorts on the South Coast fared less well. In the Spring of 1940, their piers were breached to prevent them being used by the enemy to land troops. In one episode of the popular sitcom *Dad's Army*, the platoon is marooned in the seaward pavilion of the mythical Walmington-on-Sea's pier. Like Walmington-on-Sea, real seaside towns were bombed. The line of hotels along the front of many was spoilt by a few 'missing teeth' by the end of hostilities. The beaches were covered with barbed wire, and concrete pillboxes joined the only recently built concrete coastal defences.

After the war, prospects were good for the British seaside towns. Millions again flocked to the beaches almost as soon as Germany surrendered. They brought money to spend and were anxious to make up for lost time. The fifties too, were good times for the British seaside. Even more people than in the thirties now had paid holiday and a fortnight rather than a week was becoming the norm. It was not until the sixties and seventies that cheap air flights and guaranteed sunshine began to lure people away in large numbers to Spain and further afield.

In spite of this, the British seaside has not lost its pull. A hot bank holiday still brings out motorists in droves. Perhaps it is memories of childhood; perhaps it is the spirit of carefree indulgence that goes with a trip to the seaside. There is still no better tonic than a day or two by the British coast.

Bibliography

Where works are used only as a reference for one specific chapter they are listed under that chapter. Where they have been used in more than one chapter, they are listed under the general headings as appropriate.

THE INTER-WAR YEARS – GENERAL BACKGROUND

Caffrey, Kate *'37-'39: Last Look Round,* Gordon & Cremonesi, 1978.
Graves, Robert & Hodge, Alan, *The Long Weekend, A Social History of Great Britain 1918-39*, Faber & Faber, 1941.
Seaman, L.C.B., *Life in Britain Between the Wars*, Batsford, 1970.
Stevenson, John, *British Society 1914-45,* Penguin, 1984 & 1990.
Stevenson, John & Cook, Chris, *Britain in the Depression, Society and Politics 1929-39*, Longman, 1994.

THE HISTORY OF THE ENGLISH SEASIDE

Hern, Anthony, *The Seaside Holiday: The History of the English Seaside Resort,* Cresset, 1967.
Howell, Sarah, *The Seaside,* Cassell & Collier Macmillan, 1974.
Manning-Sanders, Ruth, *Seaside England,* Batsford, 1951.
Pimlott, J.A.R., *The Englishman's Holiday*, Faber & Faber, 1947.
Walvin, James, *A Social History of the Popular Seaside Holiday: Beside the Seaside*, Allen Lane, 1978.

SPECIFIC RESORTS

Bingham, Roger K., *The Lost Resort: The Flow and Ebb of Morecambe,* Cicerone Press, 1990.
Clements, Richard, *Margate in Old Photographs,* Alan Sutton, 1992.
Clunn, H., *Famous South Coast Pleasure Resorts, Past & Present,* T. Whitingham, 1929.
Eyre, Kathleen, *Seven Golden Miles: The Fantastic Story of Blackpool,* Dalesman, 1975.
Haines, Pamela, *Hastings in Old Photographs: A Second Selection,* Alan Sutton, 1991.
Kay, Alan & Ian, *Margate: Then & Now,* Tempus, 1998.
Osborne, Rod, *The Development of Hastings as a seaside resort between 1925 and 1950 with particular reference to the influence of Sidney Little, Borough Engineer* (Unpublished thesis).
Parry, Keith, *The Resorts of the Lancashire Coast,* David & Charles, 1983.
Scurrell, David, *The Book of Margate: A Whole World of Things Memorable,* Barracuda Books Ltd, 1982.
Turner, Brian & Palmer, Steve, *The Blackpool Story.*
Whyman, J., Stafford, F. & Scurrell, D., *Margate: A Resort History, 1736-1986* Margate Charter Trustees, 1986.

SPECIFIC CHAPTERS

An Official Guide

Nash's Pall Mall Magazine, July 1937.
Numerous period guidebooks, official and otherwise.

Sun, Fun and Crowds

Automobile Association, The, *The AA Handbook 1938.*
Clunn, Harold P., *Two Days in Brighton, Queen City and Paris of the South,* 1925.
Eyre, Kathleen, *Seven Golden Miles: the Fantastic Story of Blackpool,* Dalesman, 1975.
Greene, Graham, *Brighton Rock,* first published Heinemann, 1938.
Mass Observation, 'So this is Blackpool', *Picture Post,* July 1939.
Parris, Matthew, *The Great Unfrocked: Two Thousand Years of Church Scandal,* Robson, 1998.
Phillips, Sir Percival, 'Bournemouth or the Lido?', *Daily Mail,* 1928.
Turner, Brian, & Palmer, Steve, *The Blackpool Story.*
White, Antonia, 'Brighton', *Picture Post,* August 1939.

The Remote and Unspoilt

Cole, Beverley & Durack, Richard, *Railway Posters 1923-1947,* published for the National Railway
    Museum, York, by Laurence King, 1992.
Mais, S.B.P., *The Cornish Riviera,* Great Western Railway, 1928.

Travelling in Style

Cole, Beverley & Durack, Richard, *Railway Posters 1923-1947,* published for the National Railway
Museum, York, by Laurence King, 1992.
Sutton, Richard, *Motor Mania: Stories from a Motoring Century,* Collins and Brown, 1996.
Royal Automobile Club, the, *The RAC Tour around Devon & Cornwall,* thought to be mid-1930s.
'The British Coast and its Holiday Resorts', *The Town Planning Review,* vol. xvi no. 4 (December
    1935).

Sartorial Elegance

Costantino, Maria, *Fashions of a Decade: The 1930s,* Batsford, 1991.
Herald, Jacqueline, *Fashions of a Decade: The 1920s,* Batsford 1991.
Lansdell, Avril, *Seaside Fashions 1860-1939: a study of clothes worn in or beside the sea,* Shire, 1990.

Sun Worship

Hall, Carolyn, *The Twenties in Vogue,* Octopus, 1983.
Lancaster, Osbert, *Here of All Places,* John Murray/Readers Union, 1959.
Lansdell, Avril, *Seaside Fashions 1860-1939: a study of clothes worn in or beside the sea,* Shire, 1990.
Nature Cure Educational Foundation, The, *The Health and Nature Cure Handbook,* 1931.
Probert, Christina, *Swimwear in Vogue,* Thames & Hudson, 1981.

Concrete and Chromium Plate

Bungalows & Homes by the Sea, Beachlands, Pevensey Bay, a contemporary estate agent's brochure,
    1930s.
Harwood, Elain & Morrice, Richard, *Symposium at the Bexhill Pavilion and Tour of Bexhill & St
    Leonards,* The Thirties Society and the Pavilion Trust, 1990.
Lindley, Kenneth Arthur, *Seaside Architecture,* Hugh Evelyn, 1973.
Mordaunt Crook, J. *The Dilemma of Style,* John Murray, 1987.
Stansfield, Colin, *Beside the Seaside: A Two Day Tour of North West Holiday Resorts,* published for the
    Thirties Society, 1986 (references to the Casino at Blackpool).
Whitham, Graham, *The De La Warr Pavilion,* The Pavilion Trust, 1994.
Wilton, John & Smith, John, *Eastbourne: A Portrait in Old Postcards (Volume 1),* SB Publications,
    1990.
Yarwood, Doreen, *Encyclopaedia of Architecture,* Batsford, 1985.

The Lido

D'Enno, Douglas, *The Saltdean Story,* Phillmore.
Powers, Alan, Pivaro, Alicia, Harwood, Elain & Courtney, Julia, *Farewell My Lido, A Thirties Society Report,* The Thirties Society, 1991.

The Pier and the Picture Palace

Adamson, Simon H., *Seaside Piers,* Batsford, 1977.
Bainbridge, Cyril, *Pavilions on the Sea – A History of the Seaside Pleasure Pier,* Robert Hale, 1986.
Elleray, D. Robert, *Worthing Theatres 1780-1984,* Worthing Society, 1985.
Roe, Ken, *Dreamland Weekend – Notes from the Cinema Theatre Association visit 1998.*
Twentieth Century Society, The, *A visit to the Sussex Riviera.*

Separate Tables

Automobile Association, The, *The AA Handbooks*, 1933/34, 1937/38 & 1938/39.
Courtenay, Ashley, *Let's Halt Awhile in and around Kent, Surrey, and Sussex,* Ashley Courtenay, 1939/40.
Gradidge, Roderick, 'The Architecture of Oliver Hill', *Architectural Design'* vol. XL (1979).
Lancaster, Osbert, *Progress at Pelvis Bay,* John Murray, 1936.
'London, Morecambe, and Elsewhere' in *Architectural Review,* September 1933.
McMinnies, W.G. *Signpost,* Simpkin Marshall, 1935.
'Morecambe Hotel' in *Country Life,* November 1933.
'Palace Court Hotel, Bournemouth' in *The Architects' Journal,* 1936.
Stansfield, Colin, *Beside the Seaside: A Two Day Tour of North West Holiday Resorts,* published for the Thirties Society, 1986 (references to the Midland Hotel, Morecambe).
Walton, J.K., *The Blackpool Landlady: a Social History,* Manchester University Press, 1978.

Numerous official guide books to various resorts.

Our True Intent is For Your Delight

Butlin, Sir Billy, *The Billy Butlin Story: A Showman to the End,* Robson Books, *c.* 1982.
Thomas, Harry, *Prestatyn and District – A Pictorial Past, Volume 2,* Gwasg/Hylegayn, 1994.
Ward & Hardy, *Goodnight Campers! The History of the British Holiday Camp,* Mansell, 1986.
Wintringham, Tom, 'Holiday Camp', *Picture Post,* August 1939.

Happy Memories and Wish You Were Here

Calder-Marshall, Arthur, *Wish you Were Here: The Art of Donald McGill,* Hutchinson, 1952.
Cook, Patrick, & Slessor, Catherine, *Bakelite: An Illustrated Guide to Collectable Bakelite Objects,* The Apple Press 1992.
Kodak Museum, The, *The Story of Popular Photography,* Century, in association with the National Museum of Photography, Film and Television, 1989.

1939: the Last Season and Beyond

References drawn from above.

Index

The page numbers of illustrations are indicated in **bold** type.